A Multicultural Portrait of
Professional Sports

By David P. Press

Marshall Cavendish
New York • London • Toronto

Cover: Andrew "Rube" Foster was an outstanding African-American pitcher, a superb baseball strategist, and the founder of the Negro National League in 1920. He is shown in this picture as manager of the 1919 Chicago American Giants, one of the original eight Negro League teams.

Published by
Marshall Cavendish Corporation
2415 Jerusalem Avenue
P.O. Box 587
North Bellmore, New York 11710, USA

© Marshall Cavendish Corporation, 1994

Edited, designed, and produced by Water Buffalo Books, Milwaukee

Project director: Mark Sachner
Art director: Sabine Beaupré
Picture researcher: Diane Laska
Indexer: Valerie Weber
Marshall Cavendish development editor: MaryLee Knowlton
Marshall Cavendish editorial director: Evelyn Fazio

Editorial consultants: Mark S. Guardalabene, Milwaukee Public Schools; Yolanda Ayubi, Ph.D., Consultant on Ethnic Issues, U.S. Department of Labor

For their help in the preparation of this book, the editors would like to thank Olivia Flores, formerly of the Toledo Troopers; and Sandi Self, Librarian, Pro Football Hall of Fame Library Research Center, Canton, Ohio.

Picture Credits: © AP/Wide World Photos: 48, 57 (bottom), 58 (bottom), 59 (both); © Archive Photos: 68, 73 (both); © The Bettmann Archive: 19 (bottom), 30 (top), 39, 40, 50, 56, 60, 67 (top); © Culver Pictures: 11 (bottom); © Ewing Galloway: 24; © Negro Leagues Baseball Museum: Cover, 8, 9, 11 (top), 13 (both), 16; © Reuters/Bettmann: 33 (top), 62 (bottom), 63 (top); © UPI/Bettmann: 6, 14, 15, 19 (top), 22, 27, 30 (bottom), 31, 32, 33 (bottom), 34, 36, 37, 38 (both), 41 (both), 42 (both), 43 (all), 44, 46, 47, 49, 52, 54, 58 (top), 62 (top), 63 (middle and bottom), 64 (both), 67 (bottom), 69, 71, 72 (top), 74, 75; Jim Wend/collection of Moshe ben-Shimon: 57 (top); Jim Wend/collection of Jim Hazard: 72 (bottom)

Cover photo colored by Mike Lyons.

Library of Congress Cataloging-in-Publication Data

Press, David Paul.
    A multicultural portrait of professional sports / David P. Press.
       p.   cm. — (Perspectives)
    Includes bibliographical references and index.
    Summary: Recounts the history of discrimination against minorities and women in professional baseball, basketball, and football.
    ISBN 1-85435-661-5 :
    1. Professional sports—Social aspects—United States—Juvenile literature. 2. Afro-Americans—Sports—Juvenile literature. 3. Sports for women—United States—Juvenile literature. 4. Discrimination in sports—United States—History—Juvenile literature. [1. Professional sports—Social aspects. 2. Afro-Americans—Sports. 3. Sports for women. 4. Discrimination in sports—History.] I. Title. II. Series: Perspectives (Marshall Cavendish Corporation)
GV706.8.P74   1993
306.4'83'0973—dc20   93-10316
                                                                                                                    CIP
                                                                                                                    AC

To PS – MS

Printed and bound in the U.S.A.

CONTENTS

About *Perspectives*

Perspectives is a series of multicultural portraits of events and topics in U.S. history. Each volume examines these events and topics not only from the perspective of the white European-Americans who make up the majority of the U.S. population, but also from that of the nation's many people of color and other ethnic minorities, such as African-Americans, Asian-Americans, Hispanic-Americans, and American Indians. These people, along with women, have been given little attention in traditional accounts of U.S. history. And yet their impact on historical events has been great.

The terms *American Indian, Hispanic-American, Anglo-American, Black, African-American,* and *Asian-American,* like *European-American* and *white,* are used by the authors in this series to identify people of various national origins. Labeling people is a serious business, and what we call a group depends on many things. For example, a few decades ago it was considered acceptable to use the words *colored* or *Negro* to label people of African origin. Today, these words are outdated and often a sign of ignorance or outright prejudice. Some people even consider *Black* less acceptable than *African-American* because it focuses on a person's skin color rather than national origins. And yet *Black* has many practical uses, particularly to describe people whose origins are not only African but Caribbean or Latin American as well.

If we must label people, it's better to be as specific as possible. That is a goal of *Perspectives* — to be as precise and fair as possible in the labeling of people by race, ethnicity, national origin, or other factors, such as gender or disability. When necessary and possible, Americans of Mexican origin will be called *Mexican-Americans.* Americans of Irish origin will be called *Irish-Americans,* and so on. The same goes for American Indians: when possible, specific Indians are identified by their tribal names, such as the *Chippewa* or *Mohawk.* But in a discussion of various Indian groups, tribal origins may not always be entirely clear, and so it may be more practical to use *American Indian,* a term that has widespread use among Indians and non-Indians alike.

Even within a group, individuals may disagree over the labels they prefer for their group: *Black* or *African-American? Hispanic* or *Latino? American Indian* or *native American? White, Anglo,* or *European-American?* Different situations often call for different labels. The labels used in *Perspectives* represent an attempt to be fair, accurate, and perhaps most importantly, to be mindful of what people choose to call *themselves.*

A Note About *Professional Sports*

Part entertainment, part religious ritual, and part big business, professional sports have always been something of a paradox in America. For those of us who learned at an early age to worship at its temples, sports seemed pure, just, and apart from yet better and larger than life. The playing fields were level, the rules were fair, the best teams won, and anyone, with the right mix of skill, effort, and a smile from the gods, could rise to the role of hero. Then one day we learned that the champ was addicted, that some players took a bribe, or that the owners' and players' dispute over money might threaten the start of the season. And we realized that sports have always been a mirror of ourselves, reflecting what is not only best in our world, but also susceptible to the social ills of the day.

The history of pro sports in America parallels the history of America since the Civil War, a period that has seen American women, immigrants from Europe and Latin America, African-Americans, and other ethnic minorities struggle for civil rights and respect. In the twentieth century every major sport practiced discrimination at some point and sometimes enforced outright segregation against minorities and women. This book is the story of how minority and female athletes adapted to, struggled against, and eventually overcame these injustices.

Looking at sports history this way, the heroes and heroines are athletes who not only excel on the field, but who have changed the cultural history of their sport. Athletes like Rube Foster, the father of Negro League baseball; and Eddie Gottlieb, who turned a ragtag group of sons of Jewish immigrants into the best basketball team in the country; and Marion Motley, the African-American superstar running back who helped reintegrate professional football; and Bonnie Baker, star catcher and first woman manager in the women's professional baseball league recently featured in a popular movie; and dozens more — if you're looking for a hero or heroine, there is no shortage of them in this story.

And in the end we understand perhaps that sports come close to our original ideal after all. Though they have at times inflamed prejudices, and the cost of the struggle for equality has been great, the results have been to enrich the games with higher levels of competition and achievement and a wonderfully wide array of personalities. In achieving multicultural diversity on the field, professional sports have often anticipated and spurred on changes off the field by showing us how it is done and by helping us all to understand how it is that we become Americans.

Josh Gibson — the greatest home-run hitter in the history of Negro League baseball.

CHAPTER ONE

Making, Breaking, Faking the Color Line: The Segregation and Reintegration of Major League Baseball

Ask a baseball historian about the 1934 All-Star game, and you'll probably hear the story of the most glorious moment in Carl Hubbell's glorious career. The National League's starting pitcher, Hubbell got in trouble in the first inning when he allowed two men to reach base with no outs, Babe Ruth up, Lou Gehrig on deck, and Jimmie Foxx to follow. Rising to the challenge, Hubbell struck out all three of them, then started the next inning by fanning Al Simmons and Joe Cronin. Five Hall-of-Famers in a row. It's a great story, but it's only half the story. For as impressive as Hubbell's screwball was that day, he didn't have to serve it up to Cool Papa Bell, Oscar Charleston, Josh Gibson, Turkey Stearns, Mule Suttles, or other sluggers who played in a different All-Star game. There were two All-Star games because there were two professional baseball organizations. And there were two professional baseball organizations because baseball, America's national pastime, was racially segregated. Satchel Paige, Slim Jones, and Willie Foster were faced with the challenge of pitching to the sluggers of Negro League baseball who played the 1934 East-West All-Star Game before thirty thousand spectators in Chicago. And the story of this game is equally great. It's a chapter in the saga of baseball's struggle for cultural diversity.

Thirteen years before Jackie Robinson put on a Brooklyn Dodgers uniform and reintegrated major league baseball, African-Americans already had a rich heritage and history of baseball. Forced out of the baseball leagues in the late nineteenth century, African-Americans never quit playing the game. But discrimination and segregation required separate all-Black teams and "Negro" leagues. By 1934, with the nation's economy and industry at a virtual standstill, the Negro baseball leagues, which had collapsed just a few years earlier, were struggling to reorganize in the face of the Depression.

Two Great Traditions . . .

The 1934 Negro League All-Star game was one step of many that led to the batter's box at Ebbets Field in Brooklyn, New York, in 1947. That's when Jackie Robinson, amid intense media attention and pressure, stepped up to bat and broke major league baseball's color line. Robinson's courage and athletic talents were immense, but it is not accurate to call him the first African-American to play major league baseball. Rather, with no less courage or talent, Robinson is the player who began the merger of two great baseball traditions — the European-American heritage of Ty Cobb, Cy Young, Babe Ruth, and Dizzy Dean with the African-American tradition of the early independent Black teams and of the Negro Leagues. Half of the Hall-of-Famers who entered the majors since 1947 are African-Americans and Black Latin Americans, and there is no doubt that this merger has forever enriched baseball with a dimension of talent and personalities that it never had before.

One Common Source — Nineteenth Century Baseball

Both great traditions had a common source, nineteenth century professional baseball. Professional baseball began shortly after the Civil War as America struggled to discover what it meant to be a slave-free society. While the Union and the abolitionists won the war, the segregationists in many ways won the power struggle for late nineteenth-century America. And baseball was a mirror image of this struggle.

From 1898 until 1946, organized professional baseball in America was racially segregated. But Jackie Robinson was actually the thirty-first, and not the first, African-American to cross the color line and play integrated baseball. In 1872 John "Bud" Fowler, a spry second baseman from Cooperstown, New York, signed with the Cincinnati Red Stockings and became the first of some thirty Black players who appeared for otherwise all-white teams and leagues before the color line was firmly etched in 1898. Fowler went on to play for twenty-five years, switching teams and leagues often, and hitting a career-high .350 for Binghampton in 1887.

Moses Fleetwood Walker (middle row, far left), considered to be the first Black major leaguer, with his brother, Welday, and Oberlin College teammates, 1881.

The first baseball league was formed in 1858, and by the time it folded in 1869, it consisted of nearly a hundred loosely affiliated clubs. By 1884, however, there were eleven baseball leagues associated with each other through a national agreement. It wasn't clear yet which were to become the "major" leagues and which the "minors." Because he played for Toledo of the American Association, which later became the American League, Moses Fleetwood Walker is usually considered the first African-American major leaguer. Walker, whose brother, Welday, also played briefly for Toledo, was a catcher with a strong throw, a nimble baserunner, and a consistent singles hitter who "sprayed" the ball to all fields. Popular with fans, Walker was deeply troubled by his lack of respect from other players, and in 1908 he wrote a book about racial injustice in America. After one season with Toledo, Walker played in the International League until 1889, when he helped Syracuse to the league championship.

The first two African-American baseball stars were Frank Grant and George Stovey. Although only five feet seven inches tall, Grant was an all-around player. A second baseman, he displayed great range and a strong arm. With Frank Grant at second, he was sure to turn a base hit or two into a ground out each game. Playing for the Buffalo Bisons of the International League, he hit .325 in 1886, .366 in 1887, and .325 in 1888.

At a time when African-American players were considered controversial property and usually traded after a single season, Grant was so valuable that he became the first Black to play for the same team in organized baseball for three consecutive seasons. But his talent drew attention to the color of his skin, and Grant suffered the indignities of all African-Americans in racist baseball. He was not allowed to pose with his teammates on the Bisons for a team picture. As a second baseman, he often was spiked intentionally and unnecessarily by opposing baserunners. All dangerous hitters are subject to the brushback pitch, an inside fastball that moves the batter away from the plate and often comes close to hitting him. But a dangerous Black batter who could show up a white, bigoted pitcher was especially at risk, and when Grant came to the plate, opposing pitchers frequently served up "chin music," which means they threw at his head.

Even though Bison management wanted to field a competitive team and Frank Grant helped them do that, they gave in to the rising tide of anti-African-American sentiment and released Grant after the 1890 season. Grant played a few years with Harrisburg in the Eastern League, but faced with the same treatment, he signed on with an all-Black team, the Cuban X Giants, and continued to play for independent "Negro" teams until he retired in 1903.

The Cuban X Giants, the first of many all-African-American teams to visit Cuba.

George Stovey was the first great African-American pitcher. In 1886, he was the ace hurler for Jersey City of the Eastern League, holding opposing batters to a .167 batting average. The following year, playing for Newark in the International League, he went 34-14, a league record for wins in a single season that still stands today. An all-around athlete, Stovey also played the outfield, and he rewrote the book on how a pitcher should field his position. Until George Stovey came on the scene, if a first baseman fielded a ground ball, he would try to beat the batter to first, attempting

the unassisted putout but often losing the footrace. But Stovey had a better idea. He would dash off the mound and run toward first on any ground ball hit to the right side, inventing and perfecting the technique of the pitcher covering first on a grounder fielded by the first baseman.

The Bigots Take the Field

In 1887, in the midst of one of the finest seasons ever for a baseball pitcher, Stovey was involved in an incident that has become a turning point for professional baseball, and in some ways a turning point for America. On July 19, 1887, Stovey was scheduled to pitch for Newark in an interleague exhibition game against the Chicago White Stockings of the National League. Chicago was led by their player-manager, Adrian Constantine "Cap" Anson, the biggest baseball star of the nineteenth century. A below-average fielder, Anson was nevertheless baseball's first superstar, the first batsman to get three thousand hits and the first pro to earn ten thousand dollars per year. As manager he took the White Stockings to five pennants, and his influence on and off the field was significant. Cap Anson was also a bigot. Bellowing, "Get that nigger off the field," Anson refused to allow the White Stockings to play unless Stovey was benched. To avoid a confrontation, Stovey feigned an illness and withdrew from the lineup.

Baseball's acceptance of African-American players had been an uneasy one — a result of the unresolved conflict between integrationists and those who would ban Blacks from baseball (and society). From the moment of the Cap Anson-George Stovey incident, the bigots won control of the game. By 1889, there were only three African-American players on "integrated" professional teams, and by 1892, except for two brief moments in 1895 and again in 1898, baseball had become racially segregated and would remain segregated until April of 1946.

The Rise of the Great Independent African-American Teams

In 1896 the U.S. Supreme Court made a stunning, historic ruling. The court stopped short of affirming the right of individual states to make slavery laws, but it reversed much of the social progress that had resulted from the Civil War by declaring that states did have the right to pass laws that required racial segregation. This ruling, known as *Plessy vs. Ferguson*, had two effects on baseball. For one, it validated the racist attitudes of Cap Anson and emboldened his followers. Even though baseball never passed a written rule banning African-Americans, it would be fifty years before the unofficial color line in major and minor league baseball would be crossed. The second effect of *Plessy vs. Ferguson* was the mass migration northward of African-Americans who sought escape from the segregation laws of the southern states. Among these freedom-seeking migrants were hundreds of talented baseball players and millions of baseball fans who made the organization of the Negro Leagues possible in 1920.

But the heritage of Black baseball begins long before the Negro Leagues were formally organized. There was an all-Black professional baseball team in Philadelphia as early as 1882, but the first Black team to command the

Faking the color line

John McGraw had an idea. It was a bit outrageous, and it probably wouldn't work, but that wouldn't stop McGraw from giving it a try. It was 1901, and he had just been named to manage the new American League Baltimore Orioles franchise. With a brilliant playing career behind him (he hit over .321 for nine seasons in a row), he was about to embark on a Hall-of-Fame career as a manager. He would go on to lead the New York Giants to twenty-one first- or second-place finishes in twenty-nine years.

McGraw, a brilliant strategist who was color blind when it came to baseball talent, never supported baseball's ban on Black players, and he was forever testing the waters to see if the league was ready to let him get away with signing African-Americans. McGraw also was keenly aware of the double standard baseball had toward people of color. While banning African-Americans, it cautiously accepted Indians and light-skinned Cubans, and for many years his star catcher was John Tortes "Chief" Meyers, a Cahuilla Indian and .290 lifetime hitter. It was this very double standard that led McGraw to hatch his audacious plan in 1901.

The Orioles' prospects weren't good in 1901. They needed talent, and they needed it badly. That's when McGraw discovered Charlie Grant, a young second baseman of immense talent. The only problem was that Grant (shown above in a posed photo "fielding" a "ground ball") was African-American and he had played with the all-Black Page Fence Giants and Chicago Columbia Giants. But Grant was light skinned, and with his cooperation McGraw spread the story to sportswriters that Grant was really Charlie Tokahama, a Cherokee Indian. For a while, the ruse worked until Charles Comiskey, president of the White Sox, recognized Grant and blew the whistle.

Charles Grant went on to enjoy a fifteen-year career with the Columbia Giants, Cuban X Giants, Philadelphia Giants, and New York Black Sox, but never did get to play for a major league team.

notice of sports fans and writers was the Cuban Giants. Formed in 1885 as a team of waiters from a resort in Long Island, New York, the Cuban Giants soon evolved into a popular, independent team playing 150 games a year. Most of the games were against college and semi-pro teams, but occasionally they played a highly publicized contest against a minor or major league team. In 1887, they lost a 6-4 squeaker to the National League champion Detroit Tigers when a ninth-inning error let in two unearned Detroit runs.

The team, by the way, wasn't Cuban at all. It originally took its name to avoid potential conflicts with the Cap Ansons of the world. By a weird twist of racist "logic," many who opposed the integration of Blacks and whites in baseball were tolerant of integration among whites, American Indians, and Latin Americans. So when this team of African-American waiters hit the road, they chattered gibberish on the field, hoping it sounded like Spanish and trying to pass themselves off as Cubans. The ruse proved unnecessary and unsuccessful, but the name stuck. So popular were the Cuban Giants that there were soon all-Black teams throughout the East, Midwest, and even the South.

Players on all-Black teams earned from twelve to twenty dollars a week, but without formal contracts team loyalty was almost non-existent, and the decades before the birth of the Negro Leagues in 1920 were a period of growth and experiment for Black baseball. Just as the players switched teams annually, so did the teams themselves undergo change, often rising to glory and disbanding within a few years, or switching hometown affiliation. The most consistent features of the teams were that most called themselves *Giants*

John McGraw, the major league manager who didn't care whether talented ball-players were Black or white.

(the Cuban Giants, the Cuban X Giants, the Columbia Giants, the Philadelphia Giants, the Lincoln Giants, and so on), and that the number of teams kept growing. Increasingly, these teams were challenging each other, with the winner often claiming a mythical "colored championship," but there was still the occasional series against the white major league team. All-Black teams usually fared well in these series, often winning at least half of each set.

In 1910 the Detroit Tigers traveled to Cuba to participate in a twelve-game mini-league against teams made up of Cuban and African-American players. The Tigers, featuring Hall-of-Famers Ty Cobb and Wahoo Sam Crawford, won seven, lost four, and tied one. Cobb and Crawford had a fine "season," hitting .371 and .360 respectively, but three African-Americans, John Henry Lloyd (.500), Grant Johnson (.412), and Bruce Petway (.390), led the league.

Among the many great players who matured during this era when few statistics were kept to measure careers, perhaps the most important were Sol White, José Mendez, John Henry Lloyd, and Andrew "Rube" Foster.

Sol White was not only a great player who hit over .300 lifetime and played every position on the field except pitcher, he also managed one of the best Black teams of all time, wrote a significant book, *The History of Colored Baseball* (1906), and promoted white/Black baseball games until his death in 1948. But Sol White's most important contributions were as a manager and historian. In 1902 White was hired to manage a new team, the Philadelphia Giants. He recruited Rube Foster, Charlie Grant, Home Run Johnson, and other greats, and by 1905 he had developed the Philadelphia Giants into one of the best teams in all of baseball, white or Black. And all the while he was playing and managing through those early years, White was taking notes and keeping a journal. In 1906 he published his book, which is the the first of its kind and the only surviving record of the pioneer years of African-American baseball.

In the winter of 1908, the Cincinnati Reds, as major league teams often did, toured Cuba for some post-season play. In their first game, they faced José Mendez, a twenty-year-old with a nervous fastball and a disappearing curve. Mendez, probably the best Cuban ballplayer who never played in the major leagues, struck out nine on his way to a one-hit shutout. Over the next few years he would post an 8-7 record against big league clubs, including three shutouts. Besides playing in Cuba, Mendez played with several authentic Cuban teams that played summer ball in the U.S. Pitching for the Cuban Stars in 1909, Mendez was nearly untouchable, going 44-2 for the season.

Cuba, of course, is a multiracial nation, and the Cuban teams were composed of both white and Black players. When they toured the United States, the Havana Stars, the Cuban Stars, and other Cuban teams played the African-American circuits, and Cuban teams and players continued to play an important role in the Negro Leagues of the 1920s, 1930s, and 1940s. Mendez was clearly good enough to play for a major league team, and John McGraw tried unsuccessfully to recruit him, arguing that as a Cuban, Mendez should be exempt from the ban on African-Americans. But it was not to be.

Two of Mendez's light-skinned teammates from the Cuban Stars, however, were signed by the Cincinnati Reds in 1911. Armando Marsans played as an outfielder for ten years with a .269 career average, and Rafael Almeida played as a utility infielder for three years. Although their signing raised hopes for African-Americans and other Latin Americans, it also caused controversy, and did not immediately open doors to other non-Anglo players.

Mendez would go on to enjoy great success as a player-manager for the Kansas City Monarchs in the Negro National League in the 1920s, but before then he starred for the most racially mixed team of all time, the Kansas City All-Nations. Organized by the white baseball executive J. L. Wilkinson, who later operated the highly successful Monarchs, the All-Nations played from 1912 to 1916 and had a lineup that consisted of African-Americans, Asian-Americans, American Indians, European-Americans, and Latin Americans.

The single best player from this era, and one of the best from any era, was John Henry "Pop" Lloyd. Recent research has uncovered statistics that are astounding. In 1912 Lloyd's hitting led the Lincolns to victories over both the New York Yankees and New York Giants. All in all, he hit a lifetime .342, including a league-leading .564 in 1928 when he was forty-four. In twenty-nine games against white big leaguers, Lloyd hit .321. He played for African-American teams for twenty-six years, twelve of them playing year-round by joining the Cuban Winter Leagues. Every team wanted Lloyd, and he switched teams twelve times in his twenty-six years.

Rube Foster is known both as the best pre-World War I African-American pitcher in baseball and as the founder in 1920 of the Negro National League, the first successful Black baseball league. More than anyone else, Foster gets credit for keeping the vision of integrated baseball alive during the period around WWI — a time when racial relations were more strained than at any time since the Civil War.

In the early years of the twentieth century, Foster pitched for many of the great Black teams, helping each to phenomenal won-lost records. As ace of the Philadelphia Giants staff in 1905, Foster compiled a 51-5 record against Black independent teams and white semi-pro teams, and two years later he led the Chicago Leland Giants to a 110-10 championship season that included a winning streak of forty-eight in a row. Foster was with the Cuban X Giants in 1903 when they challenged the Philadelphia Giants to a championship series. This showdown is now looked back upon as Black baseball's first World Series. The X Giants took the championship five games to two, with Foster pitching four of the five wins.

Sol White knew a good thing when he saw it, and the next year he convinced Foster to leave the X Giants and join Philadelphia. The 1904 championship rematched the 1903 teams, this time in a best two-out-of-three

Top: Slugger and top defensive infielder John Henry "Pop" Lloyd.
Bottom: Once hired by John McGraw of the New York Giants to instruct white pitchers, Rube Foster was an outstanding ballplayer, strategist, and founder of Negro League baseball. He is shown here with an unidentified member of an all-white team.

series. This time, Foster pitched — and won — both of Philadelphia's wins in their 2-1 best-of-three series triumph.

As great as he was as a pitcher, Rube Foster may be even more memorable as a manager and baseball strategist who swore by the bunt, aggressive baserunning, and the hit-and-run. In a legendary game in 1921, the Indianapolis ABCs were trampling Foster's American Giants 18-0 after seven innings. In a storybook comeback, Foster had his men bunt 11 times in the eighth inning. Aided by two grand slams, the Giants used brazen baserunning, spray hitting, and the bunt to tie the game — and end it — at 18 all.

A Case of Too Many Chiefs, Too Few Indians

Just as organized baseball had drawn a clear but unofficial color line, along came several highly talented American Indian players to muddy the waters. Each was popular with fans and good enough to impress teammates and opponents. Even though they were subjected to stereotyping and discriminatory treatment, they kept the door of cultural diversity open a notch and contributed to the proud tradition of the American Indian athlete.

The first American Indian to play in the majors was Lou Sockalexis, a Penobscot, who played parts of several seasons for the Cleveland Naps in the late 1890s. An excellent hitter (.313 lifetime average) with a sensational throwing arm, Sockalexis was so popular with the Cleveland fans that in a local newspaper contest they voted to rename the team the Cleveland Indians. Despite this, Sockalexis was berated by management for drinking and carrying on with white women. When he didn't recover quickly from a leg injury in 1899, he was dropped from the team and drummed out of the league.

Segregated baseball "tolerated" American Indians, and some, like teammates John Tortes Meyers and Jim Thorpe, had standout careers.

Probably the best known American Indian player from this era is also the one with the least distinguished career. After winning gold medals for both the pentathlon and decathlon in the 1912 Olympics, Jim Thorpe signed on as an outfielder for the New York Giants. Thorpe came to loggerheads with his manager, John McGraw, the same man who earlier tried to sneak Charlie Grant into the majors by disguising him as Chief Tokahama. After a rocky three years, Thorpe completed his baseball career with the Cincinnati Reds and the Boston Braves. Ironically, Thorpe was stripped of his Olympic medals when it was disclosed that he had played minor league baseball in 1909. After finishing his baseball career with a respectable .252 lifetime batting average, Thorpe went on to enjoy a Hall-of-Fame career in pro football.

A teammate of Thorpe's, John Tortes Meyers caught for McGraw's Giants in 1911, 1912, and

1913, when they won three straight pennants. He hit .332, .358, and .312 those years, but he didn't start playing in the majors until he was twenty-nine, and the strain of catching soon took its toll. He retired in 1917 after an eight-year career. A Cahuilla Indian, Meyers, like nearly every Indian athlete, was called "Chief," a nickname he sorely resented.

Another "Chief," Charles Bender, rarely objected to his nickname, though he always signed his autographs "Charley Bender." A Hall-of-Famer, Bender is the best American Indian player ever and one of the best pitchers of his era. He spent fifteen years in the majors, mostly with the Philadelphia A's, and compiled 210 wins against 127 losses and a 2.46 career ERA. In 1910, he led the league in winning percentage, going 23-5 including a no-hitter against Cleveland. The son of a German father and Chippewa mother, Bender loved baseball and went on to manage in the minors and coach in the majors when his playing days ended.

The "Other" Majors, 1920-1945

Up until World War I, semi-pro baseball leagues were common throughout America, and most major cities had a full-fledged league. But the draft decimated these leagues, and semi-pro baseball never again enjoyed the popularity it once had. Most independent African-American teams played half or more of their games against semi-pro teams, and this important source of scheduling disappeared almost overnight. But something else happened that dealt integration, in society and in sports, a serious blow. Race riots broke out in dozens of American cities. Rioting in Houston killed thirty-nine African-Americans and twenty-five whites, and thirty-eight more people died in Chicago. In the aftermath, white Americans by and large were gripped by fears of interracial athletics, many believing that a baseball game pitting a white team against a Black team might incite fans to riot in the stands.

It was these conditions, with equal strokes of luck and genius, that led Rube Foster to found the Negro National League in 1920. Although Foster died in 1930, and his league collapsed after the 1931 season, it gave rise to other leagues, and from 1920 until baseball was ready to reintegrate in 1946, African-American baseball players had a continuous, organized, major league showcase for their talents.

By bringing together the eight best African-American teams in the Midwest (the Chicago Giants,

New York Black Yankees Tex Burnett (manager), Harry Williams, Tom Parker, and Dan Wilson at Yankee Stadium. Banned from organized base-ball, African-American players formed their own teams and leagues.

The 1920 Detroit Stars, one of the founding franchises of the Negro National League. Two of the Stars' most notable players were Bill Holland and Bruce Petway (back row, far left and third from left, respectively).

American Giants, Cuban Stars, Detroit Stars, St. Louis Stars, Indianapolis ABCs, Kansas City Monarchs, and Dayton Marcos), Foster hoped that his league champs could play the major league champs in a true World Series. But he also saw his league as a temporary measure, as a step leading to the ultimate goal of integrated baseball. Jackie Robinson was one year old when Rube Foster's dream became a league.

There had been earlier attempts to organize a league for Black baseball teams, the first lasting one week in 1887, but the Negro National League was the first one that succeeded. Encouraged by the success of Foster's league, six eastern teams, including the Hilldale Club, Lincoln Giants, Bacharach Giants, Brooklyn Royal Giants, Cuban Stars, and Baltimore Black Sox, joined together in 1923 to form the Eastern Colored League. The following year, the Kansas City Monarchs and the Hilldale Club, winners respectively of the Negro National and Eastern Colored League pennants, played in a World Series. The Monarchs took the series five games to four when Monarch ace and manager José Mendez threw a three-hit shutout in the deciding game.

When the Eastern League folded in 1928, the memory of integrated baseball was thirty years old and fading, and the dream for integrated baseball in the future was dim. A new generation of baseball fans accepted the segregation of the races in baseball as traditional if not natural. African-American newspapers like the *Chicago Defender* and the *Indianapolis Freeman* kept alive the demands for equality and integration in baseball, believing that integration in professional sports would open other doors of social justice. But too few others raised their voices to condemn baseball's apartheid. Meanwhile, Babe Ruth pasted the best white pitchers in America, and no one asked how his home run totals may have been affected if he had to bat against José Mendez and Satchel Paige, Bullet Rogan and Slim Jones. No one suggested how lucky he was that he never had to face John Donaldson, who had pinpoint control and once averaged twenty strikeouts a game, or Willie Foster, Rube's half brother and generally considered the fastest lefthander in the Negro Leagues. And no one felt cheated that baseball fans were deprived of the thrill these matchups surely would have delivered.

The Second Negro National League and the Golden Age of African-American Baseball

In 1932, after the collapse of Rube Foster's Negro National League, African-American baseball was in danger of falling into total disarray. But two men, Cum Posey and Gus Greenlee, one a college-educated ballplayer-turned-manager and the other a gambler educated in the streets of Pittsburgh, reorganized the Negro National League and kept Rube Foster's dream alive.

Under their administration, Black baseball would grow into the biggest business in the African-American economy.

Cumberland Willis Posey began his baseball career as an outfielder for the Homestead (Pennsylvania) Grays in 1910, was named manager in 1916, and stayed affiliated with the Grays until he died in 1946. After the Negro National League was reorganized in 1933, the Grays became one of the dominant teams. Led by sluggers Buck Leonard and Josh Gibson, the Grays won nine straight pennants from 1937 through 1945, a dynasty unmatched by any professional team in U.S. sports history.

Posey's arch rival was W. A. "Gus" Greenlee. An element of gangsterism in the forms of a bootleg liquor industry, illegal gambling, and extortion rackets had infiltrated America in the 1920s and 1930s. And organized baseball was not immune from its influence. In 1919, gamblers conspired to "fix" the World Series, and in the '20s and '30s, Gus Greenlee, who ran a highly successful but illegal lottery known as "the numbers," used the money he made off this racket to finance one of the best baseball teams ever assembled, the Pittsburgh Crawfords. Greenlee was a capable executive and well-liked by his players, but much of the criticism directed at the Negro Leagues zeroed in on Greenlee and others like him who had underworld connections. When Greenlee reorganized the Negro National League in 1933, the Crawfords quickly emerged as the strongest team in the league. They kept that reputation until 1937 when, in trouble with the law, Greenlee lost his grip on the team and most of his players jumped to other teams or to leagues in Mexico and the Dominican Republic.

The Negro National League was a seven-team league in 1937 when it was joined by a new league, the Negro American League, to form an alliance that truly rivaled the white major leagues. The NAL consisted of midwestern and southern teams such as the Birmingham Black Barons, Memphis Red Sox, Cleveland Buckeyes, and Chicago American Giants. But it was the Kansas City Monarchs who most often rose to lead the league. The Monarchs were owned by J. L. Wilkinson, the only white owner in the original Negro National League and the man who made night baseball popular by developing high-powered, portable lights that traveled with the team.

The years 1937-46 were the Golden Age of African-American baseball. With both leagues in operation, a World Series was played every year, and even more popular was the annual East-West All-Star Game, which became the biggest African-American sports event of the year. In 1943, fifty-two thousand fans watched Satchel Paige and the West all-stars beat the East team, 2-1, despite a Buck Leonard home run. Salaries rose to about five hundred dollars per month for average players and a thousand dollars per month for stars, still less than half what their white counterparts would earn, but a vast improvement over the salaries of the 1920s. Ironically, the stability of the leagues contributed to their undoing. Executives of white major league baseball looked at the attendance at the East-West game and realized that the financial benefits of integration were potentially great enough to challenge what had become a tradition of segregation.

In 1945, after Americans of all colors united for the sake of the World War II effort, the baseball world was rocked by the announcement that Jackie Robinson of the Monarchs was signed by the Brooklyn Dodgers. Don Newcombe of the Newark Eagles, Roy Campanella of the Baltimore Elite Giants, Luke Easter of the Homestead Grays, and young stars from every African-American team soon followed, and the rosters of the Negro Leagues were suddenly fair game for any major league team willing to recruit Black ballplayers. As a result, the Negro National League folded after the 1948 season. The Negro American League continued to operate through 1960, even though the best players were continually raided by the major leagues. Among others, Hall-of-Famers Hank Aaron, Ernie Banks, and Willie Mays started their careers in the Negro American League before moving into integrated baseball.

Born Too Soon

When the doors of integration finally opened, the major league clubs mostly went for the younger African-American players with potential. For many of the great stars of the '30s and '40s, integration came too late.

It came too late for Oscar Charleston. Charleston, also known as "The Hoosier Comet" and "The Black Cobb," began his playing career with the Indianapolis ABCs in 1915, stayed active as player-manager of the Pittsburgh Crawfords until 1940, and continued as a manager in the Negro American League until he died in 1954. In statistics compiled from the Negro and Cuban leagues, Charleston posted a .353 lifetime average, and in 53 games against white major league teams he hit .318 with 11 HRs in 195 at bats. In his prime, he combined speed, power, and excellent defense. A large and proud man with a fiery temper, Charleston is reputed to have once snatched the hood off of a Ku Klux Klansman. In 1976, Oscar Charleston was elected to the Hall of Fame by a special Committee on Negro Baseball Leagues.

And integration came too late for Judy Johnson. Of all the great African-American third basemen before reintegration — Jud Wilson, Oliver Marcelle, Ray Dandridge — Judy Johnson was the best. Johnson played for two great teams, the Hilldales — who won three straight Eastern Colored League pennants in the 1920s — and the Crawfords of the 1930s, where he was a member of the Murderer's Row lineup along with Charleston, Josh Gibson, and Cool Papa Bell.

In his final game as a player, against a team of white major leaguers that included Rogers Hornsby and Jimmy Foxx, Johnson turned in a typically dazzling performance at third base, robbing Foxx of an extra-base hit in the bottom of the twelfth that would have ended the game. Johnson went on to work as a scout for the Philadelphia A's and Phillies and was elected to the Hall of Fame in 1975.

Integration came too late for James "Cool Papa" Bell. When the St. Louis Browns offered him a contract in 1951, Bell was forty-eight years old, and he turned it down. A contact hitter with little power and only an average arm, Bell parlayed his phenomenal speed of foot into superstardom. Not only was he a great base stealer, once stealing 175 bases in a single season, but because he beat out so many infield hits, his batting average was often in the high .300s. Once, in a game against white major leaguers, Bell scored from first base on a bunt, much to the amazement of Cleveland Indians catcher Roy Partee.

Integration came too late for Buck Leonard and Josh Gibson, the best one-two home run punch in the history of Black American baseball. Sportswriters from the African-American press named them the "Thunder Twins." Buck Leonard played first base for the Homestead Grays for seventeen years, and when he teamed up with Gibson, they became the league's most feared hitters batting third and fourth in the order as they led the Grays to nine straight NNL championships. Leonard fielded with almost flawless grace, and with his classic, smooth swing he hit for both average and power. Although he didn't start playing professionally until he was twenty-five, he kept playing until he was forty-eight.

When the Grays folded in 1950, Leonard played for five more years in the Mexican leagues and continued to be among the home run leaders. For ten games in 1953, he played integrated baseball for the Portsmouth team in the minor leagues and hit .333. After he retired, Leonard went on to help organize and serve as vice president of a minor league team. In 1972, he was inducted into baseball's Hall of Fame.

Despite his tragic and untimely death at the age of thirty-five, Josh Gibson was, next to Satchel Paige, the most popular African-American ballplayer of his day. Baseball fans have always loved a home run hitter, and Gibson certainly was that — as pure a home run hitter as baseball has ever seen. In thirteen seasons in the Negro Leagues, Josh Gibson won nine HR crowns and four batting titles. With the Crawfords in 1936, Gibson hit twenty homers and batted .457 in thirty-eight league games.

As a catcher, Gibson never played his position quite as well as Biz Mackey or Bruce Petway, but he played year-round, continually improved, and became defensively more than adequate. He left the Negro Leagues twice, once in 1937 to play in the Dominican Republic, where he hit .435, and again in 1940-41, when he played two seasons in the Mexican leagues. For the Vera Cruz team in 1941 he hit .374 with 33 home runs and 124 RBIs in 94 games. His .384 lifetime batting average will stand forever as the highest in Negro League history.

Negro League superstars James "Cool Papa" Bell (shown top, left, with Chicago American Giants manager Jim Taylor), who never played in the major leagues, and Leroy "Satchel" Paige, who eventually did.

The Disappearing Fastball and other Tall Tales

Usually associated with the frontier society of the American West, the Tall Tale is a humorous story filled with obvious exaggerations and occasional supernatural elements, but told with a perfectly straight face. Thanks to some of the ballplayers whose dugout story telling matched their on-the-field skills, the history of African-American baseball is rich in the oral tradition of this colorful folk art form. Here are a few examples.

On Josh Gibson's Power

You know, Josh Gibson could hit that white rat higher and farther than any man alive. Why one day back in the 1930s the Crawfords were playing in Pittsburgh when Josh stepped up to the plate and hit the ball so far and so high that everybody saw it go up, but nobody saw it come down. Everybody stood around with their necks bent up staring at the sky for ten minutes until the umpire finally does the only thing he can do. He waves his hand in a circle, declares it a home run, and gets the game to continue.

So the next day the Crawfords travel across the state for a game in Philadelphia. Josh is up when everyone hears this high-pitched whistling. The spectators and players look up to see this baseball come hurtling out of the heavens. No one was more startled than the centerfielder when, with a loud crack, that white rat just threw itself into his glove. Well the umpire looked back and forth from the sky to the centerfielder to Gibson for a full quarter of an hour before he makes the only ruling he can. With a sweep of his big hand he points to Josh and shouts, "Yer out! . . . Yesterday! . . . In Pittsburgh!"

On Cool Papa Bell's Speed

Oh, Oliver Marcelle was fast. Real fast. That's why they called him "the Ghost." But nobody could run like Cool Papa Bell. Yeah, Cool Papa could move. Satchel Paige was his roommate, and he related how many a night Cool Papa would turn off the light and be in bed before the room got dark. It took him a while though to realize that maybe he was just too fast for a human endeavor like baseball, too fast for his own good.

Cool Papa was playing for the Grays in a big game at Yankee Stadium against the New York Black Yankees. It was a tie score and the Grays needed a man in scoring position something bad. Cool Papa was at bat, and he determined that so long as he hit the ball, he was going to make it to second base no matter what. Sure enough, he drilled a sharp ground ball up the middle, and he never hesitated, rounding first and tearing toward second in a blur. Unfortunately for the Grays, Cool Papa suffered a sizable strawberry and got called out for interference when he was struck by that grounder as he slid into second base.

On Satchel Paige's Fastball

They say Nolan Ryan can throw a fastball 95 miles an hour, and they got the radar guns to prove it. And they say that Bob Feller threw a pitch faster than a motorcycle speeding at 100 mph. But Satchel Paige had a fastball that defied the laws of physical science. Satchel had four different fastballs. His bee ball hummed. His jump ball hopped. His trouble ball actually seemed to tamper with the molecular structure of the baseball itself, so that even if the batter timed it, the ball half dissolved, and he'd swing right through it. Then, for those special occasions, there was Long Tom.

Satchel was playing in the Dominican, and he was playing for Trujillo's team. Trujillo was a dictator. He had all these jails and armed guards, and he didn't bring Paige down there to lose. Well Satchel held a one-run lead, but the opposing team was pretty good, and they got the bases loaded in the bottom of the ninth with two outs and their best hitter up. Trujillo was in attendance surrounded by his armed lieutenants, and from the way he was scowling, Satchel knew he had to get this guy out. With the count full, Satchel reached back for Long Tom, and managed to find something extra.

The batter swung and missed, but the ball never showed up in the catcher's mitt. Trujillo ordered the catcher, the umpire, and the batboys to look for that ball for over an hour, but they never found it. That fastball just flat disappeared.

And even though he eventually played for the Cleveland Indians and the St. Louis Browns, integrated baseball came too late for Satchel Paige, one of the greatest pitchers and certainly the most famous personality in all of African-American baseball. Paige made his reputation by throwing the hottest fastball of any pitcher in the Negro Leagues. Playing for the Chattanooga Black Lookouts and the Birmingham Black Barons, Paige overwhelmed the competition before Gus Greenlee signed him for the Crawfords in 1932. Paige went 23-7 that year, and improved to a phenomenal 31-4 the next. And in 1934, he was the winning pitcher in the grueling East-West All-Star game.

Although his talent secured his reputation as one of the best pitchers of all time, Paige's character and showmanship made him into a living legend. During one stretch with the Kansas City Monarchs, Paige struck a blow for justice when he refused to book games in any town where the team couldn't lodge and eat. When he wasn't playing league games, he barnstormed with one team or another, and when his team played a semi-pro opponent or team of lesser talent, Paige would brashly call his outfielders off the field and then pitch, usually striking out the side and working the fans into a frenzy. For several years during the postseason, Paige pitched impressively for a team that toured with and played against a team of white major leaguers. Dizzy Dean, Joe DiMaggio, Charlie Gehringer, Bob Feller, and others all came away singing Satchel Paige's praises.

In 1948, at the age of forty-two, Satchel Paige became the oldest rookie and the first African-American pitcher in the American League when he signed a contract with the Cleveland Indians. Over two hundred thousand people showed up to watch Paige in his first three starts, and even though he only played the second half of the season, Paige finished his rookie year with six wins, one loss, and a 2.48 ERA as Cleveland won the pennant. Seemingly ageless, Paige continued in the majors for a few years, then pitched in the minors and continued barnstorming until 1967. In 1971, Satchel Paige was inducted into the Hall of Fame.

And integrated baseball came too late for the slugging Mule Suttles and the versatile Cuban, Martin DiHigo, and it came too late for the long-ball hitting Turkey Stearns; too late for strikeout artist Leon Day, too late for the great third baseman Ray Dandridge, and too late for literally thousands of veterans of African-American baseball who preceded Jackie Robinson. And not least, it came too late for the millions of Americans who never got the chance to see Bob Feller pitch to Josh Gibson, who never got the chance to see just how good the game might have been.

How to pitch a shutout when you're forty-six

In 1952, after he pitched his second shutout of the season for the American League's St. Louis Browns, Satchel Paige was asked by a sportswriter for his prescription for eternal youth. Here's the six-step program, according to Satchel Paige:

1. Avoid fried meats, which angry up the blood.

2. If your stomach disputes you, lie down and pacify it with cool thoughts.

3. Keep the juices flowing by jangling gently as you move.

4. Go very light on the vices such as carrying on in society. The social ramble ain't restful.

5. Avoid running at all times.

6. And don't look back. Something might be gaining on you.

Matchups between great players such as Bill Russell and Wilt Chamberlain became possible when the NBA integrated in 1950.

CHAPTER TWO

Teams from the Hood:
An Ethnic History of Pro Basketball

I n 1939, Adolf Hitler gloated over his army's occupation of Czechoslovakia and plotted to take over Poland, Joe Louis was the heavyweight champion of the world, and tennis star Alice Marble was about to be named the Associated Press Woman Athlete of the Year. This was also the year that a Chicago newspaper, the *Herald-American*, invited the best eleven pro basketball teams in the country to play in a "world tournament" and so began the magic of making professional basketball into a major national sport. From the epicenter of Hitler's army, the world shook with racial hatred just as basketball took its first steps toward joining football and baseball as one of the big three American sports. These two events were not as unrelated as it might at first seem.

Basketball in 1939 bore only a slight resemblance to today's NBA brand of game. First of all, there was no National Basketball Association — or any league that was national in scope. The *Herald-American* invited the best teams from the American Basketball League, a group of East Coast teams that played about thirty-five games per season, and the best teams from the more recently launched, Midwest-based National Basketball League. But teams with good reputations from local industrial leagues such as the Fort Wayne Harvesters and the Clarksburg (West Virginia) Oilers were also invited to the tournament, as were the best-known independent barnstorming teams, fives such as the all-Black Harlem Globetrotters and New York Rens, and even a pick-up team of Jewish all-stars calling themselves the House of David.

The championship game matched up the New York Rens with the Oshkosh All-Stars, who had finished second that year in the NBL. The Rens were led by their twenty-one-year-old rookie sensation, Pop Gates, while the tough and experienced Cowboy Edwards starred for Oshkosh. Each man led his team with twelve points in a game typically marked with the frequent smack of physical contact, no fast breaking and very little hard running, lots of passing, cautious and conservative shot selection — and no jump shots. Using two-handed set shots and an occasional lay-up, the Rens beat the All-

Stars, 34-25. Primitive? By today's standards, perhaps. But the game had already begun to evolve into the showcase of athletic finesse — the moves to the basket, the behind-the-back passes, and the deadly shooting accuracy of today's stars.

A Game for America's Immigrants

Not only was pro basketball played differently, but the ball itself was different than today's. It was leather and had seams. And the players were different. They were a different group of Americans. In the NBA today, 75 percent of the players are African-American. But for its first fifty years, pro basketball was a game whose participants were mostly the sons of European immigrants to America. The horrible ethnic intolerance and economic instability that fostered the atrocities of Adolf Hitler did not spring up suddenly in 1939. In the hundred years prior, 35 million Europeans felt impelled to leave their homelands and seek political tolerance, social equality, and economic opportunity in America. From 1900 to 1910 alone, 9 million Europeans came to America in search of a better life. In particular, as immigrants from Ireland and Italy, Ashkenazi Jews from throughout Eastern Europe, and Germans became Irish-Americans, Italian-Americans, Jewish-Americans, and German-Americans, participating in sports, specifically basketball, played no small role in that process.

This is not as surprising as it might at first seem. When they arrived in America, the European immigrants usually found out that the streets were not paved with gold, and the very things they sought — tolerance and a chance to earn a good living — were hard to come by. And it is no coincidence that within a generation of their arrival each ethnic group achieved a noticeable and disproportionate presence among the ranks of professional athletes. Recent U.S. history shows us that when a group is discriminated against economically — that is, when it has higher unemployment, higher marginal employment, and higher low-paying employment than most other Americans — then professional sports seem very tempting as a way out of that rut.

Many early twentieth century athletes came from immigrant families living in neighborhoods like this one in New York City.

Basketball became a pro sport in 1896, and its development parallels European immigration to America through the 1930s. Most of the first teams and early leagues were centered in eastern U.S. cities where the immigrants settled and ethnic neighborhoods arose. Nearly every neighborhood had a YMCA (Young Men's Christian Association), YMHA (Young Men's Hebrew Association), or settlement house, and every "Y" had a basketball court and sponsored a team. So for a second-generation male Jewish-American, Irish-American, or German-American, if he was good enough, playing pro basketball gave him a chance to make some money and break out of the confines of the neighborhood into the larger quilt of American experience. Their experiences as professional athletes sometimes heightened prejudice, sometimes helped eliminate it. Along the way, they became heroes to their people, and sometimes to all Americans, showing their fans how to both take pride in their heritage and participate in the diversity of American culture.

Early Basketball and the Buffalo Germans

From the time of its invention by James Naismith in 1891, basketball caught on immediately in the cities of the northeastern United States. Naismith wanted to create a game that could be played indoors during the winter months so students could stay physically fit year round and fulfill the YMCA ideal of "sound body, sound mind." By the late 1890s, much to Naismith's astonishment, dozens of YMCA teams had turned professional, principally in the Philadelphia, New York, and Hudson River Valley areas. Players were usually paid a share of the gate receipts and were lucky if they made a few dollars per game. Sometimes, in order to boost attendance, a dance would be held in the gym right after the game. This combination proved so popular that many teams continued the game-dance formula well into the 1940s. During home games in the 1930s, Philadelphia Sphas forward Gil Fitch doubled as a bandleader, and sometimes he had to put his bandleader's tux on over his sweaty uniform without showering so the dance could start on time.

In 1898, the first pro basketball league was formed, and even though it folded a few years later, it was replaced by other leagues, and the era of pro basketball had truly begun. Between 1898 and 1920, there was always at least one league in operation, sometimes three or more, usually confined to the Northeast, where the cities were close enough to make regional, interstate leagues possible. The most stable league during this era was the Eastern League, which operated continuously from 1909 until 1923 and featured such teams as the Camden (N.J.) Skeeters and the Reading (Pa.) Coal Barons.

But the best-known pro team from these early years of basketball, the first superstar team, was the Buffalo Germans. The Germans — made up of George Redlein, William Rohde, Henry Faust, Al Heerdt, Ed Miller, and John Maier, each the son of German immigrants to America — never joined a league, but instead would be on constant tour, setting up games as they went from city to city. They turned pro in 1904, and over the next twenty-nine years the Germans compiled a 761-85 record, including a stretch of 111 consecutive wins from 1908 until 1911.

A typical game played by the Germans had several features that have since changed or disappeared completely from basketball. The court was about two-thirds the size of a modern-day court. Because the leather ball had seams and laces, it sometimes bounced funny. A player could dribble, stop, then dribble again, a violation called "double dribbling" in today's game. There was a jump ball after every score, and the team's best free-throw shooter would usually shoot all the free-throw attempts for his team.

Perhaps the most striking differences were that backboards were not always standard, and the entire court was enclosed in a wire mesh or chain link cage, a twelve-foot fence that surrounded the court and stopped the ball from going out of bounds. It simply hit the cage and bounced back into play. Although the cage has long since disappeared, to this day basketball players are often called "cagers."

All of these conditions contributed to a game marked by rough play and low scores. The best players from that era shot about 33 percent from the floor and had a 67 percent success rate from the free-throw stripe compared to today's stars, who usually shoot about 50 percent from the floor and sink 80 percent of their free throws. Still, the Germans were one of the few pre-1960 teams that often scored more than one hundred points in a game. They didn't just beat their opponents, they humiliated them. It should be noted, however, that the Germans played mostly amateur, club teams, and rarely challenged pro teams from the leagues.

The Original Celtics and Basketball in the 1920s

In 1914, in the Chelsea district, a tough Irish neighborhood in New York City, a group of teenagers who hung around a settlement house got together and formed a basketball team. Little did they suspect that they were destined to become the most famous basketball team in the country. Within fifteen years not only would they rack up victories against virtually every pro team in the Northeast, but they would also bring their barnstorming brand of basketball to the Midwest and South, playing over one hundred games per year before more than a half million spectators. They called themselves the Celtics, and for a decade there was no team in America more talented or more successful. Pro basketball in the 1920s became known as the Celtics dynasty.

That first group of teens were named Morrissey, Barry, Whitty, McArdle, and O'Brien, each the son of Irish immigrants to America. But after World War I, the team remained "Celtic" in name only. John Whitty and Pete Barry stayed with the team throughout their glory years, but the Celtics of the '20s were a strong mix of European-Americans whose nicknames sometimes

Today's Boston Celtics are descended from this great team of Irish-American cagers.

announced their heritage: "Swede" Grimstead and "Dutch" Dehnert; the great Jewish forward Nat Holman; and big men Joe Lapchick and Horse Haggerty.

These Celtics tried participating in three different pro leagues in the 1920s. In the 1921-22 season they joined the Eastern League and won the championship. The following year they joined the Metropolitan League and were at the top of the standings with a 12-0 record when they dropped out because the league was financially unstable. And when the American Basketball League attempted to put together a league with a genuinely national scope, including franchises in the East (the Boston Whirlwinds and the Brooklyn Arcadians), the Midwest (the Cleveland Rosenblums and the Chicago Bruins), and the South (the Washington Palace Five and the Baltimore Orioles), the Celtics joined for the 1926-27 season (as the Brooklyn Celtics) and promptly won two straight championships.

But the Celtics did not build their reputation on league championships. As hard-working, independent barnstormers they razzle-dazzled millions of fans and spread quality basketball throughout the U.S. east of the Mississippi. After quitting the Metropolitan League, the Celtics hit the barnstorming trail in September of 1922, and during the next eight months they played an amazing 205 games, winning 193, losing 11, and tying 1. The following year they compiled a 134-6-1 record, and for each of the next two years they had similarly successful records. During these grueling but thrilling years on the road, Celtics players could earn as much as ten thousand dollars a year, about five times what an average laborer would make, and their travels brought them as far west as Fond du Lac, Wisconsin, and as far south as St. Petersburg, Florida. Most Americans, at this time, never traveled more than fifty miles from their homes.

By the end of the '20s, the Celtics enjoyed a reputation as the best and best-known pro basketball team in the country. They were not, however, invincible. In 1926, at the height of their talent and success, the Celtics split a six-game series with the all-African-American New York Rens, and they lost two of three to the all-Jewish Philadelphia Sphas. But perhaps their greatest contribution to the game is that the Celtics (today the Boston Celtics) played team basketball better than anyone else before them. Short, crisp passing, pesky defense, and high percentage shooting were their trademarks.

The Sphas, the Rens, and Basketball During the Depression

Two teams stand out from all others in professional basketball in the 1930s — the New York Rens and the Philadelphia Sphas. One was a barnstorming team of African-American players, while the other was a league team of all Jewish-American players. Both thoroughly mastered their competition. But each team's history in the 1930s tells a larger story of two American minorities.

The Renaissance Big Five, as they were officially known, won more games and played before more fans than any other pro basketball team of the 1930s. With a few isolated exceptions, the leagues were segregated and stayed that way until after World War II, but unlike organized baseball, pro basketball had no "Negro" leagues. Besides the Rens and the up-and-coming Harlem Globetrotters, there were several dozen other all-Black teams, but for the most part these were semi-pro, organizationally unstable, and just not in the same class as the Rens. And for all their strong points, the Rens had an awkward association with the rest of the basketball world. The Rens didn't barnstorm by choice. As an African-American team, they could not join any of the leagues. But league teams were eager to host the Rens because they were a great draw. So even though the leagues were segregated in the '30s, the Rens consistently played 100 games against white teams each year.

While basketball was becoming a professional sport in 1896, the U.S. Supreme Court ruled that states had the legal right to enforce laws that separated Blacks from whites in public places. Many of these laws, prevalent in southern states, were still in effect in the '30s when the Rens were barnstorming and in their heyday, so when they toured the South, finding places to sleep, eat, and even use the bathroom was often difficult. The North and Midwest were better, but there were still restrictions. The difference was that the team usually didn't have to ride as long to find a hotel or restaurant that would accommodate African-Americans.

Robert J. Douglas, an immigrant to the United States from the island of St. Kitts in the West Indies, founded the Rens in 1923. At that time, Bucky Lew, who played in the New England League in 1904, and Dido Wilson, who in 1907 appeared in the Mohawk Valley League, were the only two African-Americans to have played pro basketball. Black athletes had long aspired to careers in baseball and boxing and even football, but the Rens, with their visibility, their talent, and their success, became a model for African-American youth across the nation, and within a generation Black basketball talent would increase a hundredfold.

By 1930 the Rens had beaten every team in the American Basketball League at least once, except for the Cleveland Rosenblums, whom they hadn't played. The entire 1932 Rens line-up has been inducted into the Basketball

Hall of Fame. Douglas's roster consisted of Clarence "Fats" Jenkins, James "Pappy" Ricks, Eyre "Bruiser" Saitch, Tarzan Cooper, Wee Willie Smith, Bill Yancey, Casey Holt, and, from 1939 on, William "Pop" Gates. These men were the Michael Jordans and David Robinsons of their time. Yancey and Jenkins also played pro baseball, and Saitch was a nationally ranked tennis player. In the 1932-33 season, the Rens went 120-8, with an 88-game winning streak. They played the Celtics fourteen times that year and won eight of the contests.

After winning the Chicago world tournament in 1939, the Rens continued as a formidable team throughout the 1940s. They won the tournament again in 1943, and when faced with the team-by-team integration of pro basketball, they finally called it quits during the 1948-49 season, having amassed a proud 2,318 wins against 381 losses over the course of twenty-six seasons.

Shooting Hoops Under the Shadow of Anti-Semitism

The National Basketball League premiered in the 1937-38 season. It gradually grew in influence and stability until, in 1949, this league of midwestern teams merged with the new Basketball Association of America to form the National Basketball Association, the NBA, which continues to thrive today. But throughout the 1930s and early 1940s, when the nation was gripped by a massive economic depression and the world was ruled by powerful men who would soon be calling the shots in a worldwide war, the best league basketball in the country was being played by a circuit of eastern teams known as the American Basketball League. And the team that dominated the ABL, winning six championships in twelve years, was an all-Jewish squad called the Philadelphia Hebrews, also known as the Sphas. Prior to 1930 some of the best basketball players in the country, men such as Marty Friedman, Nat Holman, and Barney Sedran, were Jewish-Americans, but Jews could hardly be said to have dominated pro basketball. Yet, in the 1930s, not only were the Sphas one of the best pro teams in the country, but in an amazing explosion of ethnic athletic talent, Jewish players came to represent nearly half the make-up of the ABL. And this happened at the very time when Jews in Europe were being rounded up, imprisoned, and executed in mass graves, and even here in America anti-Semitic politicians were brazenly outspoken in advocating immigration quotas and discriminatory practices against Jews.

Even in the eastern cities with pro basketball teams, Jews rarely represented more than 10 percent of the population. Yet while Red Rosen, Inky Lautman, Red Wolfe, Moe Goldman, and Shikey Gotthofer were leading the Spha dynasty in the ABL, Jews were dominating pro basketball much the same as African-Americans shine brightest in the sport today. Attempts to explain this usually drew upon the common stereotypes of the day. Jews were thought to be smart but sneaky, quick thinkers who hated to get bruised, and these qualities supposedly made Jewish athletes particularly well suited for basketball. These generalizations were intended to be complimentary, but they still drew upon racial stereotypes. Harsher views saw Jews as cheapskates,

cheaters, and Christ-killers. The Ku Klux Klan attacked Jews with as much vehemence as they attacked Blacks, and Henry Ford, the founder of the Ford Motor Company, blamed Jews for the 1919 Black Sox scandal (some of the gamblers involved were Jewish) and led a campaign to put limits on the number of Ashkenazi (Eastern European) Jews allowed to emigrate to America. Sometimes the Sphas and other Jewish players were subjected to racial slurs and even physical abuse from fans who would sit courtside and burn passing players with lighted cigarettes while shouting "Jew bastard."

The real reasons that Jewish-Americans were so prevalent in pro basketball in the '30s were social, not racial, and they are not very different from the reasons that African-Americans outnumber whites in today's NBA. Most Jewish athletes came from poor neighborhoods with limited job opportunities. As is true today for other minorities, sports were seen as a way of moving past such obstacles as poverty and discrimination. Young Jewish boys had role models because Jewish basketball players of the 1920s were heroes in the Jewish neighborhoods. Basketball was the sport of choice for Jewish boys. You didn't need any fancy equipment to play, and every neighborhood had a court.

Settlement houses were community centers originally sponsored by the government and expressly designed to "Americanize" the children of immigrants. They provided English and civics classes and were usually built around a gymnasium as a way to lure neighborhood kids into the building. Sports were seen as a way to help children of immigrants assimilate into American culture, and the Sphas began as a settlement house team.

After fleeing the butchery of pogroms and genocide in Europe (top) and finding bigotry in their new home (bottom), many American Jews turned to basketball, boxing, and other sports to overcome prejudice and escape poverty.

The Sphas were organized by Eddie Gottlieb, an immigrant from the Ukraine who became the most knowledgeable basketball coach of his time and later became one of the first coaches in the NBA. But unlike the great Barney Sedran, who shortened his name from Sedransky, or Nat Holman of the Celtics, who in the 1920s was the ideal of the assimilated, Americanized Jewish athlete, the Sphas were brazenly open about their Jewish heritage. They wore the Star of David and the Hebrew letters *semech, pey, hey, aleph* (for **S**outh **P**hiladelphia **H**ebrew **A**ssociation) on their jerseys. By the mid-1920s they had already established themselves as a club to be reckoned with when, in 1926, they beat the Celtics two out of three and took both of their games against the Rens.

Throughout their ABL years, the Sphas would play as many non-league as league games. Gottlieb took his team on a midwestern tour every year around Christmas, and these appearances helped rally the ethnic pride of midwestern Jewish-Americans and to dispel the stereotypes of midwesterners who had very little social experience with Jews. Eventually, Gottlieb renamed his team the Philadelphia Warriors (later the San Francisco/Golden State Warriors), and entered them as a charter team in the NBA. By this time, his team was no longer all-Jewish, and Jewish basketball players were disappearing from the pro ranks as quickly as they had sprung up. Early stars such as Dolph Schayes and Red Holzman continued the tradition of the Jewish-American superstar, while others like Celtics coach Red Auerbach and Holzman, who went on to coach the Knicks to a championship, followed Gottlieb's lead into coaching and front-office positions. In the 1990s, Dolph's son Danny Schayes upheld a family and cultural tradition as a forward for the Milwaukee Bucks.

Jewish-American and NBA Hall-of-Famer Dolph Schayes.

The NBA, Slam Dunks, and African-American Superstars

It may be surprising to learn that when the NBA formed in 1949 it was an all-white league and that one of the strongest opponents to integration was Abe Saperstein, the owner-founder-coach of the Harlem Globetrotters. By 1949, pro-caliber Black basketball players were no longer a novelty. For a generation of African-Americans, the Rens served as role models and the college ranks were plentiful with Black hoops stars. And until '49, Saperstein had been a champion of African-American talent, building the all-Black Harlem Globetrotters into a world-class team at a time when there were precious few avenues open to Black cagers.

In the 1947-48 season, the Globetrotters piled up a fifty-two-game winning streak, including a victory over the NBL champion Minnesota Lakers. But when the Rens folded in 1948, Saperstein enjoyed a virtual monopoly on African-American basketball talent, and he was reluctant to give it up. Always the astute businessman, however, Saperstein saw the writing on the wall. That same year he began to change the style of the Globetrotters' play from straight-ahead competition to clowning and entertainment. By 1951 the transformation was nearly complete.

With the organization of the National Basketball Association, racial integration in pro basketball took an initial step backwards. The National Basketball League, which merged with the Basketball Association of America to form the NBA, began in 1937 as a loosely organized league of company-sponsored teams such as the Chicago Studebakers (sponsored by the Studebaker car company) and the Akron Firestone Non Skids (sponsored by the tire company) and independent teams like the Sheboygan Redskins and the Indianapolis Kautskys. Because of the draft and military enlistments, World

Once the best basketball team in the U.S., the Harlem Globetrotters have added elements of show business and comedy since the integration of the NBA.

War II put the already shaky league into something of a crisis. There was a player shortage.

In 1942, without much fanfare, Sid Goldberg, the Jewish coach of the Toledo Jim White Chevrolets, put together the first integrated team in pro basketball when he signed four African-Americans and six whites to his squad. After losing all four of their league games, the team disbanded by December. But Goldberg, who continued to play a role in organizing pro teams and leagues, had gotten quite an education. Taking his team to Wisconsin, Goldberg was unable to book rooms for his team or to find a restaurant that would serve them. The players slept in the team station wagon, and coach Goldberg slept in the car with them.

The Chicago Studebakers fielded an integrated team that same year. The Studebakers finished the season without having to sleep in the car, but players recall that when they played in Oshkosh the fans would shoot paper clips and other objects at them. At the end of the 1942-43 season, none of the Black players was signed for the next year.

It wasn't until the 1946-47 season that the NBL readmitted African-American players. This time, though, it was pretty big news. Pop Gates, star of the 1939 world champion Rens, and Dolly King, star of the Harlem Globetrotters, were signed by the Rochester Royals. Not only did these players have an immediate impact, but their signing spelled the beginning of the end to the Rens' and Globetrotters' monopoly on Black basketball talent.

Two years later, the NBL was in crisis again. A rival league, the Basketball Association of America, was aggressively luring many NBL stars and even entire franchises away from the NBL and into the BAA. Looking for new teams for the 1948-49 season, the NBL added the Dayton Rens, a reorganized version of the old Big Five, and they became the first and only all-Black team to play in a white league.

The BAA never integrated, and when in 1949 the two leagues ended their war by agreeing to merge into a new super league, the National Basketball Association, the battle for racial integration in pro basketball was temporarily ignored. It wasn't until the 1960s, when superstars Bill Russell, Wilt "the Stilt" Chamberlain, and Oscar Robertson became national heroes that there was an appreciable number of African-Americans in the NBA. In 1959, the St. Louis Hawks, the team that won the NBA title in 1958 with the only all-white team in the league, became the last NBA team to sign a Black player, and the league closed the decade of the '50s with a total of twenty-three African-Americans on its eight teams.

The achievements of African-Americans in the NBA (as well as in the short-lived rival league, the American Basketball Association) have been a cause for great pride in the African-American community and great enjoyment for all basketball fans. By the 1970s African-American players starred in professional basketball even more than Jewish-American players had a generation before. Blacks achieved this despite an unwritten quota system that limited them to six of the twelve roster positions on a team and discouraged putting more than three Black players on the court at a time. More than one hundred years after the abolition of slavery, African-Americans still found themselves economically and socially victimized by a racist society. As a result, many young Black men committed themselves at an early age with great diligence to achieve excellence in basketball. Even though only one in a thousand would make it, a career in pro basketball loomed as a shining road out of the ghetto. For some, it led to the Hall of Fame.

Bill Russell took that road, and he rewrote the book on how to play defense. A menacing six feet ten inches with long, quick arms, Russell showed the rest of the league how to cut off the lane and, even more impressively, how to block shots. A key member of the Celtics dynasty of the '50s and '60s, Russell also became the first African-American coach in the NBA.

Wilt Chamberlain took the road. In his first NBA game (1959), he scored forty-three points and grabbed twenty-eight rebounds. At seven feet one inch and 265 pounds, Chamberlain was like nothing the world of sport had ever seen before. He went on to score over 31,000 points and pull down 23,924 rebounds before he finished his career with the Lakers in 1973.

Oscar Robertson took the road. At six feet five inches, Robertson was one of the biggest and best of the many excellent African-American point guards in the 1960s. It's quite an accomplishment when a player can achieve a "triple double" in a game. A "triple double" means the player has at least ten points, ten assists, and ten rebounds in a single game. In the 1963-64 season, Oscar Robertson became the only player to average more than ten points, ten assists, and ten rebounds per game for an entire season.

Kareem Abdul-Jabbar took that road, and by the time he finished, they almost named the street after him. No one dominated basketball in the '70s like Abdul-Jabbar while playing for the Milwaukee Bucks and the Los Angeles Lakers. During the course of his career, the quota systems disappeared, and teams just suited up the best twelve people they could sign. By the time Abdul-Jabbar retired he topped the lists as the all-time leader in scoring and blocked shots.

Magic Johnson and Michael Jordan, David Robinson and Shaquille O'Neal have taken this same road out of the neighborhood. It's a well-traveled road now, and it's undergone many changes this century. But if you look carefully, you can still see the footprints of Al Heerdt, Pete Barry, Pop Gates, Hank Luisetti, and Shikey Gotthofer, the footprints of other Americans from special neighborhoods.

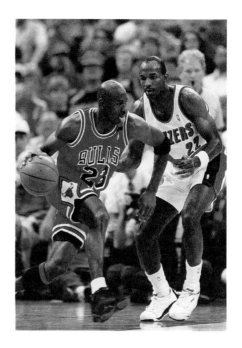

Modern NBA action: A century after the first YMCA teams hit the courts, Michael Jordan drives past Clyde Drexler (top), and Earvin "Magic" Johnson goes up against Glenn "Doc" Rivers (bottom).

Claude "Buddy" Young — sensational running back who pioneered the reintegration of pro football.

CHAPTER THREE

Lines of Scrimmage: An Ethnic History of Pro Football

His name was Claude Young, but to his fans and teammates he was "Buddy." Although he stood only five feet five inches, his speed and acceleration, his powerful legs and uncanny balance, and his remarkable ability to change direction on a dime made him a great running back. Buddy Young had many memorable games for the University of Illinois in 1944 and 1946, and for the professional New York Yankees football team in 1947 and 1948. Yes, there was a New York Yankees *football* team. They were with the All-American Football Conference, a rival to the National Football League that played an important role in the integration of pro football. But one afternoon in 1945, on a day when professional football was still very much segregated, Buddy Young, an African-American, had such a great game and made such a lasting impression on the sixty-five thousand people who saw him that professional football would never be the same. And this history-making game? It wasn't a pro game or even a college matchup. It was an exhibition game pitting a squad of sailors against a team of marines just as World War II was coming to an end.

In 1945, toward the end of World War II, Buddy Young and many top American athletes were serving in the U.S. armed services. Military commanders, in addition to doing their part in the war effort, sometimes organized base football teams to boost morale and maybe their own egos, too. Some commanders took these games so seriously that they searched the draft and enlistment files to find the names of athletes — and then they actually arranged to transfer these athletes to their base! And so it happened that in 1945, when the Navy's Fleet City Bluejackets played the El Toro, California, Marines, each team was made up of about one-third NFL players, one-third college All-Americans, and one-third better-than-average college players. This game had received so much publicity that at the kickoff there were sixty-five thousand fans in attendance, including many politicians, celebrities, and sportswriters.

Exposing an Era of Shame

Why was this game between two military bases so special? In 1945, the National Football League had been racially segregated for twelve years. And for twelve years, league officials and team owners denied that the NFL was segregated. The reason there were no Black players in the league, they claimed, was that there were no Black players good enough to make the grade. But for the people who saw Buddy Young and other African-American players perform in this game, that excuse was exposed as a racist lie, never to be believed again. And Buddy Young's performance, along with other forces that had been building, helped bring an end to this shameful period in American sports.

As the game began, most eyes were focused on Elroy "Crazy Legs" Hirsch, the All-American running back who would go on to a Hall-of-Fame career with the L.A. Rams. Most eyes were not focused on Buddy Young, but it was Buddy who stole the show. That afternoon, he returned kickoffs of ninety-four and eighty-eight yards and scored his third touchdown when he took a hand-off from scrimmage and scampered thirty yards, leading his team, the Bluejackets, to a 45-28 win.

It was not easy to reverse the intolerant practices that led up to the sorry situation of 1945, even though professional football got off to a very promising start. The first pro league, the American Professional Football Association, was founded in 1919 with Jim Thorpe, an American Indian and America's

Jim Thorpe — a great American athlete

Today's professional athletes are not the first to make controversial head-lines. When Jim Thorpe headed up the first pro football league in 1919, he had already had a good share of athletic glory and controversy. By 1912, Thorpe's achievements were legendary.

Born in 1888 of American Indian, Irish, and French ancestry, Thorpe drew national attention as a college football player and was named halfback on the All-America teams in 1911 and 1912. In the summer of 1912, Thorpe joined the U.S. Olympic squad, where he won gold medals in both the pentathlon and decathlon, a display of athletic versatility unmatched before or since. But the celebration was short-lived. Based on a brief stint playing semi-pro baseball to earn money during his college years, the Amateur Athletic Union in 1913 stripped Thorpe of his amateur status and deprived him of his gold medals.

From 1913 until 1919 Thorpe played major league baseball for several clubs, including the New York Giants and Cincinnati Reds. He also played pro football in the NFL for the New York Giants and Chicago Cardinals before retiring in 1929 at the age of forty-one.

Thorpe continued to put on some exhibitions, and he even boxed a little, but the last twenty years of his life were a slow descent into alcoholism and poverty. Before he died in 1953, he was elected a charter member of the Pro Football Hall of Fame, and in 1950, American sportswriters and broadcasters selected him as the greatest athlete of the century.

In 1983, the Olympic medals that were taken from him seventy years before were restored to his family. By then, Thorpe had been dead for thirty years.

Paul Robeson: scholar, athlete, actor, political dissident

At six feet three inches and 225 pounds, Paul Robeson had a commanding presence, on the gridiron and on the stage. He played three years in the early NFL, including 1922 with the Milwaukee Badgers, where he teamed with Fritz Pollard and Duke Slater to form the only African-American threesome in pro football before 1946. Oddly, the only reason he played pro football was to finance his law school education. Cruelly, once he got his law degree, he found precious few clients willing to hire an African-American attorney.

Born the son of a former slave in 1898, Robeson was a gifted athlete, actor, and singer who became so embittered by the racial discrimination he experienced in America that he tried to seek a better life in the Soviet Union and other European socialist countries. Although he returned to the United States in the early 1960s, and he lived to see much progress made in civil rights before he died in 1976, his life remains today politically controversial.

best-known athlete, as its president. Although the APFA folded after a year, the time was right for pro football in America, and in 1921 the National Football League began.

The Early Years — a Shaky Integration

The early NFL was a disorganized league, and it was not uncommon for teams to fold in midseason. And the early NFL, like early major league baseball, was an integrated league, although it was not well integrated and did not resemble the present NFL at all. In the NFL today, 60 percent of the starting players are African-American, and team rosters are filled with representatives of nearly every American ethnic group. Fritz Pollard and Rube Marshall were the first Black professional football players. Pollard, a running back, played for the Akron Pros of the APFA when they were league co-champs in 1920, and Rube Marshall played briefly for the 1921 Rock Island team of the new NFL. In 1922, Pollard became the first African-American coach when he organized, played for, and coached a new NFL franchise, the Milwaukee Badgers.

In all, only thirteen African-American athletes played pro football from 1920 to 1933, and there were never more than five teams in any one season that had African-Americans on the roster. No team ever had more than three Black players. The best known football player in America during this era was Red Grange, but many of the Black players competed evenly with the likes of Grange. Among the better players were Duke Slater, a premier tackle for the Chicago Cardinals; Paul Robeson, who was also a well-known actor and singer; Jaye "Inky" Williams, who played six years with four different teams; and Joe Lillard and Ray Kemp, the two last Black players before the era of segregation.

Lillard, nicknamed "the Midnight Express," was a terrific athlete who played as a kicker, punt returner, and running back for the Chicago Cardinals in 1932 and 1933. Despite his outstanding performance for the Cards and his potential for so much more, Lillard was released before the end of his second year in the NFL. Earlier in the season he and a player from the Cincinnati team had thrown a few punches, and both players were ejected from the game. The league used that incident to label Lillard a "disciplinary problem" and to justify his release.

That same year, 1933, was Ray Kemp's rookie year, and for the first time since 1928, there was more than one African-American player in the NFL. Kemp played for the Pittsburgh Steelers, and his signing marked the first time since 1926 that any team other than the Chicago Cardinals had signed a Black player. Although it looked as if the trend toward segregation might be reversing, it was not to be. At the end of the year, Kemp was cut. And then there were none.

Bigotry Drives African-Americans Out of the NFL

Actually, the league began to get rid of its Black players in the late 1920s. Some managers claimed they were protecting Blacks against the dirty tactics of bigoted players and thus dumping them "for their own good." Others claimed the players had a bad attitude. Using these and other flimsy excuses, managers methodically weeded Black players from their squads. By 1928, Duke Slater, who later became a judge in Chicago, was the only African-American player in a league of ten teams.

The driving force behind this purge of African-Americans was George Marshall, the owner of the Boston Redskins, who had become politically powerful within the NFL. Marshall was a gifted organizer, and under his guidance the NFL changed from a league where franchises opened and folded like April umbrellas to an organization with stability and structure. By example, Marshall showed other owners how to make money from an NFL franchise, and so when Marshall talked, the other owners listened. But Marshall was also a bigot who believed that Blacks and whites should be socially and athletically separate. By moving his team from Boston to Washington, D.C., then a racially segregated city, and vowing never to hire minority athletes, Marshall set the example for an all-white NFL. No other owners stood up to him, and pro football began its era of disgrace.

This unwritten ban on African-American players stayed in place throughout the years of Franklin Delano Roosevelt's presidency. This was a contradiction and an embarrassment for President Roosevelt and his administration. Roosevelt's policy for America was known as The

Bigot and team owner George Marshall (below and bottom, left, with team), who led the move to segregate the NFL. In 1962, his Washington Redskins became the last major U.S. sports team to integrate.

New Deal, and one of its key slogans was "No forgotten men, and no forgotten races." Roosevelt had good reason to support civil rights and progress for race relations. The coalition that elected him to the presidency for an unmatched four terms was based largely on African-American support, and in 1936, he captured 75 percent of the Black vote. And there *was* progress for racial equality during his administration. Influential African-Americans such as Mary McLeod Bethune, a teacher and founder of schools, received important government appointments, and First Lady Eleanor Roosevelt led a vocal attack on bigotry. But despite these gestures of government support for civil rights, two-thirds of America's Blacks still lived in the South, where rigid, often brutal policies of segregation were enforced on every part of daily life from maternity wards to cemeteries, and everything in between. And even outside the South, movies and radio depicted African-Americans in a narrow range of stereotypes. This contrast of racist traditions and progressive forces for civil change gave the country a split personality during the Roosevelt years. Unfortunately, professional football chose not to ally itself with the higher hopes and achievements of the New Deal.

In many states, laws required racial segregation in public places such as schools and bus stations.

World War II and the Fight for Equality at Home

Not everyone sat back and accepted the hypocritical double standard of "equality" for some but not for others that was becoming an unwritten rule in the NFL. Just as the plot to segregate football simmered for years before league segregation became a fact in 1933, so did the forces of reintegration begin to gather and build momentum long before the NFL finally readmitted African-Americans in 1946.

The Black press was a loosely knit network of newspapers run by and for African-American communities throughout the United States. Almost every city that had a sizable African-American population had at least one Black newspaper. Led by such papers as the *Pittsburgh Courier*, the *Chicago Defender*, and the *Kansas City Call*, and distributed effectively but unofficially by African-American railroad porters, the Black press in the 1930s and 1940s waged an outspoken and vigorous campaign against bigotry and prejudice throughout American society and especially in the arena of American sports. Journalists Wendell Smith and Ralph Mathews were among the most militant. More than once they angrily spoke out against the contradictions of a U.S. government that denounced the racism of Adolf Hitler but looked the other way when it came to discriminatory laws and practices in the United States.

Until 1948, even the U.S. Armed Forces were racially segregated.

"Before any of our people get unduly excited about saving democracy in Europe," warned the *Courier* in 1939, "it should be called to their attention that we have not yet achieved democracy here." A few years later Ralph Mathews, also for the *Courier*, went so far as to urge World War II GIs, both "colored" and white, to finish up the job in Berlin and Tokyo, then turn around and "drive out the Fascist coalition of Southern Democrats and Republicans who are trying to Nazify America." By the time of Buddy Young's performance for the Fleet City Bluejackets, prominent white journalists such as NBC sportscaster Sam Balter and *New York Daily News* columnist Jimmy Powers had joined voices with the Black press to demand opportunity and recognition for African-American athletes.

By the mid-1940s, claims that there were no African-Americans good enough to play NFL-calibre football rang hollow, and the traditions that had kept the NFL segregated were about to crumble. World War II and the rise of rival professional football leagues delivered the final blows. One impact WWII had on the Americans who lived through it was that it challenged segregationist ways of thinking and behaving. After working and fighting alongside people of color, white Americans were more receptive than ever before to the changes of civil rights, including the integration of sports. Also, during the war, so many NFL players enlisted or were drafted that league management was forced to consider the practical side of integration. They needed the talent, and there wasn't enough white talent to go around. But rather than look for African-American players, team owners temporarily sidestepped the issue by reducing the size of the rosters from thirty-three to twenty-five players.

Nothing Like a Little Competition to Stir the Pot

More than anything else, it was the launch of several semi-pro and fully professional leagues in the mid-1940s that brought Black players back into professional football. Even though all of these leagues eventually folded, they set an example for the NFL and made it possible for pro football to become a truly American sport. One of these leagues, the Pacific Coast League, was regional, but the United States Football League and the All-American Football Conference were national in scope. Announcing plans for the league in 1944, USFL president Red Grange declared that the league would be open to Black athletes. Unfortunately, the USFL folded before it ever played a single game. The AAFC, with better financial backing, did become a reality.

Disappointingly, it was an all-white league when it began in 1945.

In 1946, however, an important showdown took place in Los Angeles city hall. Two L.A. football teams, the Rams of the NFL and the Dons of the AAFC, petitioned to use L.A. Municipal Stadium for home games. The city of Los Angeles, influenced by a group of African-American journalists, took a stand denying use of the facility to any team practicing

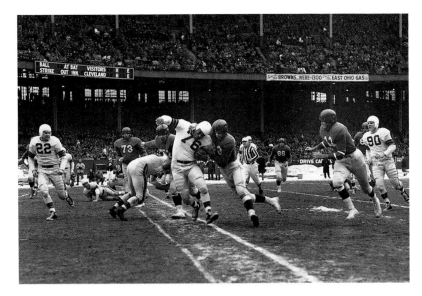

racial discrimination. Although both teams promised to sign Black players, the Rams kept their promise and the Dons did not, at least not at first. And so, in 1946, reluctantly, because the Rams needed a place to play and had no other choice, the NFL became reintegrated for the first time since 1933. They purchased the contracts of Kenny Washington and Woody Strode from the Hollywood Bears, but neither player saw much playing time.

It was up to the AAFC, in particular the Cleveland Browns and their coach, Paul Brown, to lead the way in recruiting African-American athletes into pro football. Paul Brown showed the sports world that not only was signing Black players the right thing to do, but it was good coaching. In 1946 he signed Bill Willis and Marion Motley, both of whom were named first team

Soon after the NFL reintegrated, African-Americans such as Marion Motley (above, #76) and Dick "Night Train" Lane (below) rose to superstardom and Hall-of-Fame careers.

all-pro as they helped lead the Browns to the first of four consecutive league championships. Spurred on by Cleveland's success (and despite the slap of Willis and Motley having to sit out the Miami game because of a Florida state law forbidding interracial athletics), the AAFC charged ahead, signing ten more Black players in 1947. By 1948, only two AAFC teams, the San Francisco 49ers and Baltimore Colts (which had moved from Miami), remained segregated.

Breaking Through to Equality in the NFL

In the NFL, the reluctantly integrated Rams didn't exactly blaze a trail toward equality in their league. The Detroit Lions signed two Black players in 1948, but it was not until the AAFC folded in 1950 that integration in the NFL really got under way. When the Cleveland Browns and several other former AAFC franchises joined the NFL, they brought their integrated talent with them. And in 1950, when Marion Motley led the league in rushing, and the Browns, the most integrated

team in the league, won the division, the advantages of fielding an integrated team were apparent to everyone.

The corner had been turned. By 1960, 12 percent of the league players would be African-American. But progress was slow, and not without conflict and resistance. In 1962, George Marshall's Washington Redskins became the last team to integrate. Even then, it was not until after a string of losing seasons and the personal intervention of President John F. Kennedy, who was embarrassed that the nation's capital should be represented by the only all-white team in the nation. Among the many great Black players who began their careers in this era were several future Hall-of-Famers, including Joe Perry, Roosevelt Brown, Dick "Night Train" Lane, Emlen Tunnel, Ollie Matson, and, of course, Jim Brown, probably the best running back the game has ever seen.

Gale Sayers, O.J. Simpson, Walter Payton, Tony Dorsett, Earl Campbell, and other Hall-of-Fame-bound superstars continued the tradition of the African-American running back throughout the '70s and '80s. But where were the Black centers, offensive guards, linebackers, punters, kickers, and most conspicuously, quarterbacks? Today African-Americans are better represented at these positions. But could it be that racial stereotyping blocked the appointment of African-Americans to starting assignments at the "thinking-man's" positions? Nowhere is this question better answered than in the history of the Black quarterback.

Back in 1953, an African-American player named Willie Thrower took a few snaps as quarterback for the Chicago Bears, and in 1968, Marlin Briscoe

Outspoken athlete and social activist Jim Brown (top), and Joe Perry (bottom), one of the first to break pro football's color line.

played most of the season at quarterback for the Denver Broncos, then of the American Football League. But Briscoe was soon moved to wide receiver, and by the early 1970s, the lack of a Black quarterback in the NFL became an issue of controversy. All attempts to rationalize the "no Black quarterback" phenomenon sounded sickeningly like the explanations given for segregated football in the '30s and '40s. One by one, each African-American candidate for quarterback was cut or switched to another position. Throughout the 1970s, great athletes were disqualified for "bad knees," "throwing too hard," "a lack of speed," and other suspect reasons. The truth is that while the football establishment had come a long way in acknowledging the physical talents of African-American athletes, prejudicial habits and old racist ways of thinking worked against the acceptance of Black athletes at positions of team leadership. Clearly, the first starting African-American quarterbacks would have to be exceptional in every way.

Doug Williams came out of a terrific college career at Grambling to join the Tampa Bay Buccaneers in 1978. By 1980 he became the first African-American to regularly start at quarterback in the NFL. Warren Moon was a standout at the University of Washington, but he chose to sign with the Canadian Football League, where he set passing records and won player-of-the-year honors before joining the Houston Oilers in 1984.

And so one by one the prejudices are exposed as lies, and each time African-American athletes fulfill the legacy of Buddy Young and Joe Lillard before him, and participate more fully in pro football. In 1990, Art Schell of the Raiders followed up a Hall-of-Fame playing career to become the first Black man to coach an NFL team since Fritz Pollard did it briefly in 1922. With the appointment in 1992 of Dennis Green as head coach of the Minnesota Vikings, the

NFL had two African-American coaches, and another door was opened.

With integration, pro football has become more competitive, more exciting, and more entertaining. It has become a sport that all Americans can watch with pride because it is a sport that does not exclude any Americans. And this story of African-American athletes — men who overcame second-class citizenship, who overcame discrimination and exclusion from the league, and who overcame prejudice to rank among the greatest stars the league has known — inspires us all.

Top: Willie Thrower, the NFL's first African-American quarterback. *Middle and bottom:* Great Black running backs of the 1960s and 1970s Gale Sayers and O.J. Simpson.

Dorothy Harrell, Chicago Colleens. Women's pro baseball soared
to prominence in the 1940s before fading a decade later.

CHAPTER FOUR

Leagues of Their Own: Women's Pro Baseball, Basketball, and Football

A late summer's night, 1946. Once in a while, a cool breeze freshens the humid night air. The war is over. Millions of American GIs have returned stateside to reclaim the jobs they gave up when the war began. And symbolic home front heroine Rosie the Riveter has been asked to put down her rivets and rattle those pots and pans. Meanwhile, at Horlick Field in Racine, Wisconsin, an extra-innings baseball game stands at a tense, scoreless tie.

It's the championship game, pitting the team from Rockford, Illinois, against the Racine nine. In the top of the ninth, Winter, the Racine fireballer, surrenders up two singles and walks one, but gets the slugger Kamenshek to fly out with the bases loaded to retire the side. In the bottom of the ninth, Morris, the Rockford hurler, paints the corners and strikes out the side to keep a no-hitter intact. But sensing his ace is starting to tire, Rockford skipper Bill Allington goes to his bullpen and pulls Morris in favor of relief specialist Deegan. Deegan's control and speed are the best in the league, but Racine baseruners have enjoyed some success running against Rockford when Deegan is on the mound. In the bottom of the fourteenth, they get their chance.

With the score still deadlocked at nothing-nothing, Kurys, who leads the league in base-stealing, leads off with a solid single, a frozen rope to left. With Trezza up next, the strategy wheels spin. The Rockford infield plays at double-play depth and tries to anticipate Racine's move. Sacrifice? Hit-and-run? After three consecutive pick-off attempts, Deegan fires some high, inside heat that sends Trezza reeling backwards off the plate. Kurys bluffs a steal and draws a throw down to first. The next pitch, a curve that starts inside, backs the wary Trezza away from the plate, but breaks over the inside corner for a strike. On the next pitch, Kurys breaks for second. It's an outside fastball that Trezza swings at and misses; the throw is a good one, but Kurys slides in just ahead of the tag, paying the usual price of a scraped thigh.

Now Deegan gets just a bit careless. Her curve ball hangs over the plate a moment, and Trezza cracks a sharp grounder through the right side of the infield. Kurys never hesitates, and tears around third toward home.

The Game of the Year

Baseball fans could not ask for a better, more thrilling ending to a championship game, and no one who was there could ever forget it. It was, perhaps, the most exciting moment to date in the history of women's professional team sports in America. Sophie Kurys beat the throw, and the Racine Belles beat the Rockford Peaches one to nothing for the title of the 1946 All-American Girls Professional Baseball League.

More than five hundred players, ranging in age from fifteen to thirty years old, including fifty to sixty Canadians, played major league women's baseball in the United States from 1943 through 1954. The league that showcased the skills of these athletes, the All-American Girls Professional Baseball League, was the longest-running and most successful organization of women's professional team sports in U.S. history. But the twelve-year history of the AAGPBBL does not change the fact that no religious, ethnic, or racial group has met with as much discrimination and lack of opportunity in professional sports as have women.

Feminine Ball Tossers and Bloomer Girls

In order to understand why women have had and continue to have so little opportunity in the world of pro sports, it helps to examine some of the longstanding beliefs and practices that have restricted roles available to women throughout U.S. history. It is no small contradiction that a great democracy like the U.S. did not grant women the right to vote until 1920. For two-thirds of the nation's history, half of its citizens could not vote simply because of their sex, and it was commonly believed that women could not reason well enough to exercise the vote properly. Nor were misconceptions about women limited to underestimating their powers of reason. Physically, women were believed to be naturally frail and ill-suited for activities requiring physical expertise. The medical establishment at the turn of the century promoted as fact the notion that physical activity could be detrimental to women, and at their urging, separate sets of rules were made for sports and for "girls'" sports. Perhaps most disturbing and

Smashing any stereotypes about "feminine frailty," Sophie Kurys of the Racine Belles hook slides safely into third.

damaging of all was the derision suffered by those women who participated in and excelled at sports despite all the social disapproval. They were often victims of personal attacks on their character and tasteless jokes about their sexuality.

The surprise, then, is not that there were so few professional women's teams prior to World War II, but that there were any at all. It's downright astonishing that several teams were so talented and accomplished that they were in a league of their own. Like the 1927 Yankees or Joe Louis in his prime, they just outclassed everyone else in their field.

We know that women college students at Vassar played some form of baseball as early as 1866 because there is a record of the townspeople becoming upset and trying to put a stop to it. Another newspaper account of 1875 reports a game played by "feminine ball tossers" for gate money, so women's professional baseball dates from almost as far back as men's pro baseball. There seems to have been a loosely organized network of touring teams throughout the 1880s, and in 1890, an entire women's pro baseball team was arrested for playing a game on a Sunday before two thousand paying spectators in Danville, Illinois, which, like many towns, had "blue laws" banning entertainments on the Christian Sabbath.

By the 1920s, barnstorming women's softball teams, known as "bloomer girls" because of their uniforms, became quite common. The Philadelphia Bobbies were the best known, most talented, and most legitimate of them all. They even toured Japan in 1925 and contributed to the budding popularity of baseball in that country. Edith Houghton, signed at the age of fourteen to play as the Bobbies' shortstop, later became the first woman scout for major league baseball. Under the guidance of sleazy male promoters, other bloomer-girl teams had less of a competitive and more of a burlesque mission. Touring under such names as the "Num-Num Pretzel Girls" and "Slapsie Maxie's Curvaceous Cuties," they usually played all-men's teams and often played off the public stereotypes about women athletes by fea-

The woman who struck out Babe Ruth

Kenesaw Mountain Landis, the strong-willed, almost tyrannical commissioner of baseball, was just furious. Even if it was only a publicity stunt, Landis would have nothing to do with it. He hadn't been this enraged since the last time an advisor suggested he reconsider the unofficial ban on racial integration in the major leagues.

In 1931, a minor league baseball team, the Class-A Chattanooga Lookouts, signed Jackie Mitchell, a seventeen-year-old woman, to a pitching contract. Lookout management saw a great opportunity when they scheduled an exhibition game with their parent club, the New York Yankees. On game day, Mitchell was on the mound for the Lookouts, and Yankee legends Babe Ruth and Lou Gehrig were in the lineup for the Bronx Bombers. Mitchell struck them both out.

Ruth and Gehrig no doubt agreed to strike out, but it was all done in the spirit of focusing attention on the Chattanooga team and on Mitchell's talents. Landis moved quickly. Declaring that "life in baseball is too strenuous for women," the commissioner voided Mitchell's contract and reprimanded the Yankees. With considerably less fanfare, Alta Weiss and Elizabeth Murphy played long and very successfully for men's semi-pro softball teams, but major league baseball would have none of it. In 1952, the major leagues adopted a statute barring women from signing as players with men's teams.

Hazel Walker, who starred for the All-American Redheads in the 1930s and 1940s, continually broke her own women's free-throw shooting records and regularly defeated male challengers during half-time contests.

turing a cigar-chomping, wig-wearing male short-stop in drag. The serious woman athlete who wanted to play ball and earn a living had little choice but to put up with these humiliations.

Prior to WWII, basketball provided one of the few other professional opportunities for team-sport women athletes. Next to the Globetrotters, perhaps the best-known novelty-act, barnstorming basketball team was the All-American Redheads. Organized in 1936 by veteran basketball entrepreneur Ole Olsen, the Redheads continued playing until the 1980s, and for a while the organization was so successful that there were three Redhead teams touring at the same time.

The Redheads always played men's teams, usually semi-pro or amateur teams, and they won 80 percent of the time. In their heyday, the Redheads would play 185 games during a six-month season, sometimes touring Mexico and the Philippines as well as the United States. Much like the Globetrotters, the Redheads combined straight-ahead basketball skills with an ingenious assortment of trick plays. Despite these concessions to show business, the Redheads maintained a high standard of athleticism and dignity, and they served as role models for a generation of basketball-playing American girls and women who would go on to make up the rosters of two professional women's leagues in the 1970s and 1980s. But it wasn't until World War II and the formation of the All-American Girls Professional Baseball League that women — white women, at least — had their first, full-fledged opportunity to participate in a legitimate league of professional team sports.

RBI Rosies and Women's Baseball

When the U.S. entered WWII, baseball team owners and national leaders met to discuss the role major league baseball should play in the war effort. Many thought that baseball and all professional sports were unimportant during the crisis of war and that baseball should suspend its schedule until after the war was over. Others, including President Franklin Roosevelt, successfully argued that it was baseball's patriotic duty to boost the morale of U.S. citizens on the home front. Still, many team owners worried. With so many players drafted, others enlisting, and still others quitting the game to serve in war-related industries, the quality of the game might suffer. More to the point, so would attendance. With this possibility weighing heavily on his mind,

In 1948 Chicagoans could brag about one more baseball team — the Colleens. Despite the fact that the Cubs and White Sox would follow the lead of the Brooklyn Dodgers and add African-Americans to their rosters, and despite a reported tryout of two Black women for the South Bend Blue Sox, the AAGPBBL decided against making the leap into integrated baseball.

Chicago Cubs owner, businessman, and patriot Philip K. Wrigley proposed the formation of a women's professional baseball league.

In 1943 there were a thousand women's softball teams within a hundred-mile radius of Wrigley Field in Chicago, and softball had enjoyed a decade as the number one participatory sport in America. From the thousands of amateur players on those teams, Wrigley's scouts found sixty of exceptional ability, and in 1943 his dream became a reality. That first year, the new baseball league consisted of four teams based in Racine and Kenosha, Wisconsin; Rockford, Illinois; and South Bend, Indiana.

The number of teams grew to a high of ten in 1948, but shrank back to five by the time the league folded in 1954. Some teams, like the Milwaukee Chicks and the Chicago Colleens, were one-year franchises, while others, the Rockford Peaches and the South Bend Blue Sox, lasted the entire life of the league. Although the league started with underhand pitching and a large ball, it gradually evolved into a game very much like men's baseball with a nine-inch hardball, overhand smoke from the pitcher's mound, and eighty-five-feet base paths (men's baseball has ninety-feet base paths). Each year, the league needed about thirty to forty new players, but as the game changed and became less and less like softball, it was harder to find women's softball league stars ready to make the jump to the AAGPBBL. Despite the need for more talent, the league never followed the major leagues in signing Black players.

At its peak, the league had a 126-game schedule, plus playoffs, and attendance figures topped a million. The league already showed signs of growth and increased popularity when Wrigley sold it at the end of the second season. While Wrigley had run the league as a nonprofit organization, the new managers were determined to make money off the enterprise. Meanwhile, the first season ended successfully, with the Racine Belles coming out on top after a 54-game schedule that attracted nearly 200,000 fans.

Ladies' Charm School and the Suicide Squeeze. When 5 million U.S. women, most of whom had never held salaried positions before, took jobs

Rosie the Riveter — symbol of the ideal U.S. woman during WWII.

between 1940 and 1945, Americans reacted with mixed emotions. On the one hand there was the ideal of Rosie the Riveter: strong, muscular, patriotic, bravely stepping in to fill an important and needed role, and doing it willingly and well to the cheers of her countrymen and women. On the other hand, many felt that it was unfortunate and distasteful that women had to leave the home and take jobs that men were better suited to hold, and that as soon as the war was over, this situation should be reversed. In 1943, the national Parent-Teacher Association passed a resolution urging mothers, "for the sake of their children," to resist the temptation to take a job.

From the start, AAGPBBL executives were sensitive to these mixed feelings, and they determined to project a feminine and "ladylike" image of the players. Fearing the raised eyebrows and jokes about women athletes and their lack of femininity that were common in the past, these league executives, all of them men, passed rules that governed the design of the uniforms, the off-field behavior of the players, and the appointment of chaperones to each team. These same executives also required attendance at charm school for the players and even made an attempt to ban the use of nicknames.

Fortunately, the rule banning nicknames was unenforceable. Although public address announcers were instructed to introduce players by their full, proper names only, the local sportswriters, the fans, and all the players knew each other by colorful nicknames. Alma Ziegler was "Gabby," Senaida Wirth was "Shoo Shoo," Lavonne Paire was "Pepper," Dorothy Harrell was "Snooky," Loretta Lipski was "Sticks," and so forth. Unfortunately, for the players at least, the league's other rules were not as easy to sidestep.

"It was hard to walk in high heels with a book on your head when you had a charley horse," observed the power-hitting catcher Pepper Paire. But that is exactly what league vice president Arthur Meyerhoff had the players doing for the first few seasons. Meyerhoff hired Helena Rubinstein, a nationally-known operator of a chain of beauty parlors, to run a mandatory course in good grooming and "ladylike manners" each spring training. After a few years, the charm school was dropped, but the league continued its efforts to feminize its players through a booklet, "A Guide for All-American Girls: How to Look Better, Feel Better, Be More Popular."

Charged with enforcing the guidelines of this booklet were the team chaperones. The first chaperones were most often gym teachers, but as the league went on, chaperones were increasingly drawn from the ranks of retired players. Unsuitable, which meant "unladylike," behavior was contractually forbidden by the league, and often it was the chaperone's almost impossible job to enforce these rules. While men's major league baseball players were endorsing beer and cigarettes, the AAGPBBL players were forbidden to smoke or drink alcohol in public. Players had a curfew, and all dates had to be OK'd by the team chaperone. In fact, players could be fined fifty dollars for appearing "unkempt" in public and ten dollars for arguing with an umpire during a game. For someone salaried at fifty-five dollars a week, these fines were stiff but did little to stop the frequent and highly theatrical brouhahas with the men in blue.

Skirting the Issue. The league's obsession with the image of its players is nowhere more obvious than in the design of the uniforms. Basically, the women were required to play in short skirts, hemmed six inches or more above the knee, with gym shorts underneath. From the spectator's point of view, the uniforms were certainly pretty. They made for a good photo opportunity. They showed a lot of thigh. For the players, the main problem with these uniforms was sliding. In a game where stealing and aggressive base running were so essential to success, most of the women found it necessary to slide forty or more times each season. But because of the design of their uniforms, each player had twenty inches of exposed flesh from knee to upper thigh, and most of the women played with open scrapes and abrasions on their legs.

The league produced many fine players and a handful of great ones. Dottie Kamenshek, first baseman for the Rockford Peaches, led the league in batting in '46 and '47 and went on to become perhaps the league's best hitter before being slowed down by a back injury. The best all-around athlete the league had known was Gabby Ziegler, the middle infielder and spark plug for

With a bat in her hand and a song in her heart

Lavonne "Pepper" Paire joined the All-American Girl's Professional Baseball League in its second season and soon made a lasting impression as a catcher, a slugger, and a curfew-breaking free spirit. Paire played hard, and she suffered the first major injury of the league when she fractured her collarbone while applying a tag in a home-plate collision.

Paire also emerged as the unofficial league balladeer, and she wrote the AAGPBBL "Victory Song," a tune that became an anthem of sorts for the players.

The AAGPBBL Victory Song

Batter up! Hear that call!
The time has come for one and all
To play ball. For we're the members of the All-America League,
We come from cities near and far.
We've got Canadians, Irishmen and Swedes,
We're all for one, we're one for all,
We're All-American.
Each girl stands, her head so proudly high,
Her motto Do Or Die.
She's not the one to use or need an alibi.
Our chaperones are not too soft,
They're not too tough,
Our managers are on the ball.
We've got a president who really knows his stuff,
We're all for one, we're one for all,
We're All-American!

OK. So maybe it's not "Take Me Out to the Ballgame." But Paire's tune captures the patriotic mission and comaraderie of the All-American Girl's Professional Baseball League.

To this day, when the players get together for an occasional reunion, they still sing this song.

His mother was Ted Williams

She stood a mere five-foot-one, but she had a mean batting eye. She rarely swung at a pitch out of the strike zone, and when she did swing, she rarely missed. Her name was Helen Callaghan, and they called her the "female Ted Williams." In 1944, at nineteen, Callaghan (shown above, center, with two of her Minneapolis teammates) left her home in Vancouver, British Columbia, with her sister, Margaret, to join the AAGPBBL and become one of its early stars.

The 1992 hit movie *A League of Their Own* is based loosely on the experiences of the Callaghan sisters. While the real Ted Williams earned $100,000 a year, the female Ted Williams made between $50 and $100 a week. Still, this was more than her father, brother, or husband were likely to earn back in Vancouver. Callaghan loved the game, but played for only four years, leaving the league to raise a family. One of her sons, Kelly, became a filmmaker, and his 1988 documentary on the AAGPBBL focused renewed attention on this all-but-forgotten league. Another son, Casey Candaele, went on to play major league baseball. A scrappy utility infielder for the Houston Astros, Candaele is known for his fine defensive play and competitive spirit. In an age when the Ken Griffeys, senior and junior, and Bobby and Barry Bonds receive so much publicity, Casey Candaele is the only major leaguer whose mother played professional baseball.

In December of 1992, after a long battle with breast cancer, Helen Callaghan Candaele St. Aubin died.

the Grand Rapids Chicks. Ziegler joined the league in its second year and played for eleven years until the league folded. She could bunt, steal, and turn a double play as well as anyone who ever played in the AAGPBBL. Bonnie Baker, long-time catching star for the South Bend Blue Sox, was instrumental in breaking the $100-a-week salary cap and in 1950 became the league's first full-time female manager when she took the reins of the Kalamazoo Lassies. Despite lifting the team from last to fourth place, during the off-season the league directors inexplicably passed a resolution banning female managers except on a temporary, emergency basis.

The Decline and Fall of the AAGPBBL. Perhaps the most poignant moment in AAGPBBL history came early in 1944. The league had a patriotic mission to entertain citizens on the homefront and keep spirits high. Sometimes games wouldn't start until 11:00 P.M. so that second-shifters from the local defense plants could watch the games. Men and women in service uniforms were admitted for free, and each game began with the players marching onto the field in the V-for-Victory formation for the playing of the national anthem. It was in just such a charged atmosphere in 1944 that Milwaukee Chicks catcher Dorothy Maguire learned only moments before the game that her husband had been killed in action. Overcome with grief and tears, Maguire assumed her place in the V-for-Victory and then played the game.

When WWII ended in 1945, the league continued to thrive for several years and actually didn't peak in popularity until 1948. But the original conditions that had spawned the league — the patriotism and unified war effort, the funneling of young men out of the work force and into the armed services, the need for women to leave the home and enter the traditional "man's world" — faded from the fabric of everyday American life, and the league lost much of its reason for being and entered a period of decline. When the AAGPBBL began, Americans were being urged to cooperate with rationing, buy war bonds, give blood, work hard, and make personal sacrifices for the war effort. By 1950 the new pitch was for Americans to buy an automobile, a home in the suburbs, and a futuristic gizmo called a television. As millions of veterans returned to civilian life, millions of women left the work force, many to raise a family. Inflation hit, and labor unions struck for higher wages.

Among the tiny, unpopulated atolls far out in the Pacific Ocean, the U.S. was testing its pride and joy, the atomic bomb, while a cold war with the Soviet Union was heating up. These and other changes took their toll on the AAGPBBL. Many players chose to retire in favor of marriage and family, and replacements were hard to find. The game played in the AAGPBBL had become less and less like softball, and so women's softball league stars were less ready to play the AAGPBBL game. At the same time, softball's popularity as a recreational league sport declined. And inflation reduced the appeal of AAGPBBL salaries. In 1952, it wasn't easy to convince a woman athlete to leave her home and play baseball in the Midwest for a hundred dollars a week. Faced with dwindling talent and attendance, the league folded after the 1954 season.

Women's Pro Football and the NWFL

It's the 1970s, and the teams come and go, into and out of such far-flung places as Cincinnati, Buffalo, Pittsburgh, Toledo, Oklahoma City, San Diego, Albuquerque, San Antonio, Houston, Cleveland, Santa Fe, New York, Dallas, Chicago, Fort Worth, Detroit, Los Angeles, and San Jose. The teams also play in Erie, Pennsylvania, and Middletown, Dayton, Akron, and Columbus, Ohio, and in Tulsa and Lawton, Oklahoma. Their names are lively and colorful, and some, such as the Dandelions, Dolls, Fillies, Bluebonnets, and Herricanes, are a bit more feminine-sounding than team members might like.

The sport is women's pro football, and its heyday spanned the 1970s, when a group of teams pooled their resources to form the National Women's

Star running back Linda Jefferson (# 42) led the Toledo Troopers to the 1973 NWFL title.

Football League. For the most part, NWFL games attracted fans that numbered more often in the hundreds than in the thousands, and the media often played up the novelty of women playing a "man's game" over the legitimate athletic contests on the field. Not surprisingly, the papers focused on subjects that had nothing to do with football, such as how "pretty" or "petite" a "lady" fullback might be, or whether a quarterback "cried" when she was sacked. And even when they did write about the game itself, reporters often seemed more interested in the players as "gals" than as athletes. For example, one magazine writer who was otherwise enthusiastic about women's football could not resist describing how the ball "bounced around in the flanker's dainty palms, which were all rough and red, but not from using the wrong laundry detergent."

Scrambling for Respect. Despite this kind of frivolous attention, the NWFL also received some serious coverage, especially when the league held championship games or drew large crowds. In 1973, nearly three thousand fans watched the powerful Toledo Troopers defeat the Dallas Bluebonnets, 37-12, in the first women's pro football game in the Southwest. The victory was Toledo's twelfth in a row, while the Bluebonnets were playing their first game ever. In another game, eight thousand fans turned out to see the same two teams compete, and six thousand fans once watched Toledo claim the league championship from its archrivals, the Oklahoma City Dolls.

Even with a league to draw up schedules and generate publicity,

Women in football: famous firsts and lasts

In 1970, a big "first" took place: the appearance of a woman on a men's football team. "Pigskin" Pat Palinkas broke the gender line as a place-kick holder with the Orlando Panthers of the Atlantic Coast Football League. On her very first play, the 122-pound Palinkas fumbled the snapped ball and was clobbered by 240-pound tackle Wally Florence of the Bridgeport Jets. Florence was neither impressed nor amused by his place in history: "I tried to break her neck. I don't know what she's trying to prove. I'm out here trying to make a living, and she's out here prancing around making folly with a man's game." Meanwhile, the other key player in the incident, the place-kicker himself, happened to be Pat's husband, Steve. When he was cut from the team after two games for poor place-kicking, the Palinkas-Panther relationship was no longer a family affair. And when Pat missed several practices because of publicity tours and TV appearances, she, too, found herself cut from the active squad.

the franchises came and went, usually numbering between eight and twelve teams, and in the '80s the loosely organized league folded completely. But without the NWFL and such high-profile franchises as Toledo, Dallas, and Oklahoma City, women's football probably would have gotten even less of the attention and respect which it deserved — and which the players demanded. In fact, when the president of the NWFL suggested taking a "Harlem Globetrotter approach" and turning the league into a bunch of novelty teams, the players unanimously vetoed the idea, telling him they wanted their football to stay "strictly legit."

But certain factors — the lack of formal training among most NWFL players, the level of play itself, which was often likened to that of a boy's high school program, and the players' salaries — led many observers and players to question how "professional" the NWFL actually was. Unlike softball, which provided a training ground for the women who played baseball in the AAGPBBL, football provides virtually no formal training system for bringing girls and women up through the ranks. And so, while some girls may have played neighborhood football, usually with brothers and boys their own age, most stop playing by the time they turn teenagers, when football suddenly becomes a "man's game." Boys move on to freshman football, and girls get out.

As Pro as It Gets. Players' salaries were nothing to brag about, either. *When* the players were paid, the salaries were strictly double-digit — usually not more than twenty-five dollars per game. But because of their love for the game and spirit of camaraderie, most teams played for "fun and expenses," as one Toledo Trooper put it — and they certainly showed themselves to be "professionals" in their attitudes and dedication.

Over the years, the fans and media who followed the NWFL found that the quality of play had improved and that the league boasted serious star-quality players. Of these, by far the most widely recognized was Linda Jefferson, the famed running back of the Toledo Troopers. Generally acknowledged as the most talented woman to play in the NWFL, or in any professional women's football game, Jefferson compiled statistics most NFL players would envy. In one season alone, she ran an average of eighteen yards every time she carried the ball and scored thirty-five touchdowns. By the time her career ended in the late 1970s, she had scored more TDs than any other pro player, male or female, including the legendary all-time NFL leader, Jim Brown.

These numbers, her enthusiasm for the game, and her general athleticism in football and other sports earned Jefferson a host of news interviews and speaking engagements. They also added publicity and respect to the exploits of her fellow female gridders — and a bulging file of clippings buried deep in the library of the Pro Football Hall of Fame.

Future Fields of Dreams? The history of the NWFL is neither long nor particularly glorious. But it came at a time when the women's movement was

More than a case of pre-game jitters

Sharon Calhoun, offensive guard for the San Jose Ravens, had been feeling ill lately. When she found out that she was pregnant, she managed to find humor in her season-ending situation. "I'd played several games," she said, "so naturally everyone said we ought to be penalized for having too many people on the field at one time. I told them the baby thought we were playing Canadian rules. They use a twelfth man, you know."

The Educational Amendments Act of 1972

"No person... shall, on the basis of sex, be excluded from participation in, be denied the benefits of, or be subjected to discrimination under any educational programs or activities receiving federal financial assistance." This sentence, known as Title IX of the Educational Amendments Act, requires athletic programs at schools receiving federal funding to provide equal opportunity and benefits to women as they do to men. At the time this act was passed by the U.S. Congress in 1972, only 2 percent of the athletic department budgets at colleges nationwide was spent on women's sports. Father E. M. Joyce, vice president at Notre Dame University, immediately blasted Title IX as asinine. At the time, his school awarded $1 million annually in scholarships and financial aid to male athletes, and nothing at all to women athletes. After twenty years of legal challenges and heel-dragging from within the NCAA establishment, Title IX has succeeded in increasing funding for women's athletics to 25% of the total budgets.

Women began playing competitive basketball soon after the sport was invented.

beginning to make its presence felt in many walks of life in the U.S., and thus the men and women who contributed to the league were pioneers in ways that went beyond the gridiron. In addition to providing yet another field of competition for female athletes, the NWFL caused many people to rethink their usual ideas of what games and goals were "proper" for girls and women. The NWFL also gave birth to discussions in print and elsewhere about how football could be made to accommodate women, instead of the other way around. For example, in 1975 a female journalist suggested that women's and men's football "merge" without having sexually integrated teams on the playing field at the same time. Women's squads might compete with one another during the first and third quarters, for example, while men play the second and fourth, as in roller derby. This would also add a dimension to football as a spectator sport, with more women turning to the game as fans, particularly in front of TV sets at home.

The time for this idea has apparently still not come. And yet, as that writer also suggested in 1975, the very existence of a women's football league, along with each player, each female camera operator, and each producer who may have televised a game or two — each of these people may have stood for "one small victory . . . one woman who was doing something she was capable of, and something she enjoyed." And despite the setbacks that have befallen women's football in the years since the NWFL, perhaps such small victories will have paved the way for a time when we can accept any person wanting to do what he or she does best, regardless of gender, color, or competence, and cheer them on without being shocked by — or dismissive of — their achievements.

Women's Pro Basketball

Since the mid-1950s a wave of change has swept through the rules and attitudes of both U.S. society at large and women's athletics in particular. The decades of the 1960s and 1970s and 1980s were characterized by social movements: the Civil Rights movement, the counter-cultural movement, the anti-war movement, a gay rights movement, and the women's movement. Each phrase refers to a loosely organized, grass roots swelling of citizens who advocated change and often protested against traditional ways. The changes that these movements set in motion have been legal ones and political ones; they have changed the ways we think, and they have changed the ways we behave, and they are still going on today. But without the network of amateur, collegiate, and semi-pro leagues needed to develop the talent, it is unlikely conditions have changed enough to make another women's professional baseball or football league possible right now. Conditions are certainly ripe for a women's professional basketball league, however, and it is shocking and disappointing that Americans are being robbed of such a rich source of athletic entertainment.

Not a Priority? Sports and basketball have not been the primary focus of the women's movement. Equality in the work place remains the number one demand. But changes in women's athletics have paralleled the strides made by women in our larger society.

Women's basketball in the mid-1950s was little more than an intramural sport. There were some inter-school games, but there were no tournaments, no championships, and virtually no records kept. There were six players to a side who played a half-court game. On offense, players could only bounce the ball twice before they were required to shoot or pass, while on defense players could not "steal" the ball by slapping it out of the offensive player's hands. All of these rules were vestiges of a time when it was believed that strenuous athletics were dangerous to a woman's health. Thirty years later, women's basketball had evolved into a quick-moving, full-court game nearly identical to men's basketball. It became a fully-funded collegiate sport complete with All-America selections and national tournaments, and an Olympic sport. And significantly, there had been several attempts to establish a bona fide pro league.

The WBL — Big Time at Last? The Women's Basketball League (WBL) got off to a promising start when eight thousand fans turned out on December 9, 1978, to watch the Chicago Hustle outshoot the Milwaukee

Above: A collector's item — a WBL T-shirt. *Below:* Carol "The Blaze" Blazejowski of the New Jersey Gems.

Top: When the WBL and WABA folded, many athletes like Teresa Edwards (#32) pursued successful pro careers in Europe. *Bottom:* Nancy Lieberman played on men's and women's teams.

Does 92-87. Disappointingly, due to poor marketing, flagging fan interest, and the inability to land a television contract, the WBL collapsed after three seasons.

Like the AAGPBBL and the NWFL, the WBL was organized by male executives and managed by male coaches. That first season saw eight teams play a thirty-four-game schedule. The New York Stars won the championship, but attendance for the league averaged only 1,500 per game. The franchises from Dayton and Minnesota folded before the end of the season.

Salaries that first year ranged from a low of five thousand dollars to a high of fifteen thousand dollars, but rose much higher the second season when the league got its first true superstars. African-American Luisa Harris dominated at the position of center. Six feet three inches and incredibly strong, Harris was a three-time All-American for Delta State who averaged thirty-one points and fifteen rebounds per game in her junior year before joining the Houston Angels of the WBL. Carol "The Blaze" Blazejowski starred for the New Jersey Gems after a college career at Montclair State College (N.J.) that saw her lead the nation in scoring in her junior and senior years. The biggest star was Ann Meyers, New Jersey Gems star and WBL Most Valuable Player. Meyers, whose brother David also played pro basketball, was the first four-time All-American and was even drafted by the Indiana Pacers of the NBA.

The only person to win both Woman Athlete of the Year and Jewish Athlete of the Year honors is Nancy Lieberman. Speaking of her youth, when she learned to play basketball in Long Island schoolyards, Lieberman says, "I never knew that other girls were playing basketball. I had always thought of myself as one-of-a-kind. My family and friends had tried to discourage me from playing. They said I had no future and that I would never go to college and grow up to be a nice young lady." What she did do was become a member of the 1976 Olympic silver medal team at the age of sixteen, lead Old Dominion to two national championships, and take her improvisational street style to the WBL, where she starred for the Dallas Diamonds in the league's final season. When in 1984 the Women's American Basketball Association tried to build a new league out of the ashes of the WBL, Lieberman was there to lead the new Dallas Diamonds to the ill-fated league's only championship. The WABA folded after its premier season.

Is There Life After the WABA? Although there have been no professional league opportunities since the WABA, there continue to be more talented women basketball players than ever before. It is difficult for them to find ways to earn a living as an athlete, however — at least in North America. There are women's professional basketball leagues in Spain, Italy, Germany, Scandinavia, and Japan, and it is estimated that some five hundred American women are currently playing professional basketball in Europe and Asia. Several, such as Teresa Edwards and Katrina McClain, earn more than $100,000 for a six-month season, more than anyone ever made in the WBL or WABA. For those who prefer to stay in the U.S., many are talented enough to play in semi-pro men's leagues. After the WABA collapsed, Lieberman went on to play for the Long Island Knights, a minor league basketball team, then toured with the Washington Generals, the straw man team that plays against the Harlem Globetrotters.

Lynette Woodard played briefly in a pro league in Italy, where she led all scorers with a 31-point-per-game average; but she is better known for following up a brilliant college career as the highest scoring female athlete in history by becoming the first female member of the fabled Harlem Globetrotters. With talents such as Lieberman and Woodard, and more recent college standouts Yvette Larkins, Tarcha Hollis, Michelle Burden, Tine Freil, Andrea Congreaves, Genia Miller, Jan Jensen, and others, it is apparent that the talent exists for another professional women's basketball league.

Above: Lynette Woodard, the first woman selected to play with the Harlem Globetrotters.
Below: Tampa Bay Lightning goaltender Manon Rheaume, the first woman to play in any of the four major pro sports leagues.

The Future: Hockey and Other Shots on Goal

It is also clear that as women get the chance to play sports and develop their skills at an earlier age, the talent gap between men and women continues to get narrower and narrower, especially in those sports that depend less on pure strength and more on hand speed and coordination. In 1992, a female goalie, Manon Rheaume, was signed by the National Hockey League's Tampa Bay Lightning to play with the Atlanta Chiefs, its affiliate in the International Hockey League. In her first game, there were nine shots on goal, and she had seven saves.

Regardless of Rheaume's future, the future of professional team sports will undoubtedly be increasingly coed. As more and more women athletes can perform competitively with the best men, the old misconceptions about the frailty of women will have less and less influence over who gets to play, and one day, a single rule may even apply to all athletes, men and women alike: the best players suit up.

The signing of Jackie Robinson — a turning point for baseball, pro sports, and U.S. society.

CHAPTER FIVE

The Jackie Robinson Revolution

I n America's community of committed integrationists, the 1947 signing of Jackie Robinson to a Brooklyn Dodgers contract set off a celebration unlike anything since the Emancipation Proclamation. It was a momentous turning point not only for baseball, but for all American sports and beyond, injecting hope for freedom and equality in every corner of American social and political life. Within the next few years professional football and basketball became integrated, and even the American Bowling Congress, the Professional Golfers Association, and the United States Lawn Tennis Association would drop their bans on African-American members. In 1948 President Truman integrated the U.S. Armed Forces, and six years later the Supreme Court ruled that public schools, and the athletic facilities in those schools, must be available to all Americans. While it is perhaps an exaggeration to credit the signing of Jackie Robinson with the end of segregated education in America, it is undeniable that hundreds of professional athletes followed Robinson's lead. In the 1960s, when America was shaken by the Civil Rights Movement, frequently it was these same African-American athletes who walked the picket lines and helped oppose continuing discrimination in sports and society.

The fight for equality in the sports world has in no way been limited to the big league team sports. Significant battles have been fought in boxing rings, on tennis courts, golf courses, and other fields of play. And no discussion of multiculturalism in professional sports would be complete without highlighting the contributions of Jack Johnson and Joe Louis, Arthur Ashe and Billy Jean King, Lee Elder and Nancy Lopez, and other athletes who pushed the racial, ethnic, or gender limits of their sports. In this chapter, we will look at the strides made in these sports. We will also look at the fruits borne by the Robinson revolution in the arena that Jackie Robinson affected most profoundly: post-segregation major league baseball.

Beyond Baseball — Tennis and Golf

Professional tennis and golf have strikingly similar racial and ethnic histories. Unlike basketball, which became the sport of choice for working-class

Star Hispanic athletes such as Pancho Gonzales (top) and Chi Chi Rodriguez helped tear down racial segregation in tennis and golf.

immigrants and the urban poor, tennis and golf were the recreational sports of the white upper classes. Until the 1950s, both the United States Lawn Tennis Association (USLTA) and the Professional Golfers Association (PGA) practiced segregation and excluded African-Americans from membership. And like organized baseball, both sports used a twisted form of racist logic to sanction and embrace an occasional athlete of color, thus showing how "broadminded" organization officials were at the same time they practiced discrimination. In the late 1940s and early 1950s, when African-Americans were still trying to get access to USLTA tournaments and facilities, Mexican-American Pancho Gonzales captured the hearts of tennis fans and dozens of tournament championships on his way to becoming the number-one ranked player in the world. And even though the PGA did not repeal its "Caucasians only" clause until 1959, Chi Chi Rodriguez used golfing talent and a flair for showmanship to become a fan favorite in the 1950s and lead the way for other Hispanic golfers, including Lee Trevino and Nancy Lopez, who ranked among the best in the world in the 1970s and 1980s.

Despite these upper-crust origins, tennis and golf were not reserved exclusively for the leisure class. Early in the twentieth century, middle-class Black Americans showed increasing interest in these sports, and as early as 1916 the American Tennis Association (ATA), the African-American counterpart to the USLTA, was founded and dedicated to promoting tennis in African-American communities and building courts and facilities. With a similar mission, the United Golfers Association (UGA) ten years later began crowning African-American golf champions.

The best players from those early days were Ora Washington and Eyre Saitch in tennis and Robert Ball and Lucy Williams in golf. Washington won eight ATA women's titles in the 1930s, and Saitch also starred for the Renaissance Big Five basketball team. Both Ball and Williams were repeat winners of the UGA National Tournament in the 1930s. But with limited or no access to the manicured courts and professional facilities, and drawing athletes mainly from the limited pool of affluent African-Americans, the ATA and UGA did not spawn the kind of talent or interest witnessed in Negro League baseball. It wasn't until the Jackie Robinson revolution that things began to change.

In 1950 at the age of twenty-three, Althea Gibson struck a double blow when she became the first African-American to play at the USLTA Nationals at Forest Hills, the most prestigious tournament in the U.S. at one of its most exclusive country clubs. Growing up hard in the New York City neighborhood of Harlem, Gibson not only integrated professional tennis, opening the doors for Arthur Ashe and other African-Americans, but she focused much needed attention on women's tennis, and in many ways made it possible for Billie Jean King, Martina Navratilova, Chris Evert, and others to become superstar athletes. By 1958, Gibson had won the Women's Singles title at Wimbledon twice and rose to the number-one ranked female player in the world.

Women's tennis received its next big boost from an exhibition match in 1973 when Billie Jean King defeated Bobbie Riggs, once a world-class pro who had won Wimbledon and the U.S. Open. The match was brashly publicized as a "battle of the sexes," and when King won handily in straight sets, women's tennis was taken more seriously than ever. Later that year the U.S. Open became the first major tournament to offer equal prize money to the men's and women's division titlists. King went on to further the cause of women's sports by serving as an organizer and charter member of the short-lived but coed World Tennis League, and by publishing *WomenSports*, a magazine dedicated to coverage of women's athletics.

Martina Navratilova (top), Billie Jean King (above), Arthur Ashe (left), and other tennis stars of the 1970s and 1980s owe much to Althea Gibson, the African-American woman who integrated pro tennis.

Versatile athlete and pioneering woman golfer Mildred "Babe" Didrickson Zaharias (top), and Charles Sifford (bottom), who led the way for other African-Americans into the PGA.

A true beneficiary of Althea Gibson was Arthur Ashe, the first African-American male athlete to rise to the top ranks of pro tennis. Ashe won the U.S. Open in 1968, the Australian Open in 1970, and Wimbledon in 1975 before suffering what seemed the cruel misfortune of heart disease, forcing his retirement at the age of thirty-six. The blow seemed even crueller when it was learned that during subsequent bypass surgery Ashe had contracted the Human Immunodeficiency Virus (HIV). But although his playing days were over, this same misfortune freed Ashe to redirect his life. In the thirteen years between his retirement and his untimely death of AIDS in 1993, Ashe wrote the definitive study of Black American sports history, *A Hard Road to Glory*, and served tirelessly as an activist and fundraiser for such organizations as the American Heart Association, the United Negro College Fund, Artists and Athletes against Apartheid, and the Arthur Ashe Foundation for the Defeat of AIDS. He knew he was suffering from a fatal disease, but he played out his match, leaving tennis and the world the gifts of this bright, sensitive, talented athlete.

Perhaps more than any other sport, professional golf stubbornly resisted integration and social progress. Even the Ladies Professional Golfers Association (LPGA), formed in 1948 to validate and promote the sport made famous by Mildred "Babe" Didrickson Zaharias, barred Black women from membership, and it wasn't until 1967 that Renee Powell became the first African-American woman on the LPGA tour. Until 1959, the only acceptable role for an African-American in the PGA was as a caddy to the white golf pro, a direct and decadent vestige of the slave-slaveholder relationship.

The best African-American golfer in the U.S. at the end of World War II was Charlie Sifford. A former caddie, Sifford became a six-time winner of the UGA National Tournament, and he even played successfully in a few integrated tournaments in Canada and the U.S. before finally getting a PGA membership card in 1959. Ten years later he became the first African-American golfer to win a major event when he captured the 1969 Los Angeles Open. Sifford was often harassed during tournaments, not by other players, but by racist spectators who would shout epithets and even throw beer cans at him as he was about to swing. But he persevered and made it possible for other Black golfers to follow. In 1975, Lee Elder became the first African-American golfer to play in the prestigious Masters Tournament in Augusta, Georgia. And for the four-year period 1981 through 1984, the winningest player on the PGA tour was an African-American, Calvin Peete.

Perhaps the best-known golfer in the 1950s wasn't a professional; he was President Dwight Eisenhower. Although he did much to popularize golf, he never spoke out or showed any interest in addressing the sport's racial injustice. But even without leadership from the top, segregated pro golf fell before the unstoppable progress of the Jackie Robinson revolution.

The Bomb, "the Bambino," and *Besuboru*

World War II came to an explosive end in 1945 when the United States dropped atomic bombs on the cities of Hiroshima and Nagasaki, forcing Japan to accept unconditional surrender. But the U.S. almost ended the war with a Babe Ruth home run instead.

Ruth was immensely popular with the Japanese, dating back to 1934, when he toured Japan with a team of American All-Stars, delighting the baseball-hungry Japanese by belting fourteen homers in seventeen games. Despite the war, "the Bambino" remained such a popular figure in Japan that the U.S. government hatched a secret plan that called for Ruth to make a series of radio broadcasts urging the Japanese people to surrender. We'll never know for certain if it would have worked. For better or worse, war strategists decided to use the bomb instead of the Bambino.

After Ruth's visit in 1934, the Tokyo Giants, Japan's first professional baseball team, was formed. But the events of World War II set Japanese baseball back on its heels. Seventy-two pro players were killed, and many of the ballparks were bombed out or converted into farmland during the war. But like the Japanese economy and spirit, Japanese baseball, or *besuboru,* came back stronger than ever after the war.

Japanese baseball differs from American baseball in a few ways. The baseball is just a little bit smaller, but home plate, and the strike zone, are six inches wider. Games can end in a tie, and ballpark dimensions are smaller, with home run fences averaging about twenty to thirty feet shorter than most American stadiums.

In part because of these differences, Americans have been reluctant to return the respect for Japanese players that the Japanese have had for American stars. Superstars of Japanese baseball have included Sadaharu Oh, who hit 868 home runs, more than Hank Aaron, in a twenty-two-year career, and Sachio Kinugasa, who played 2,215 consecutive games (more than Lou Gehrig) for his team, the Hiroshima Carp. But Americans have looked upon these achievements with suspicion, just as they have distrusted the achievements of American big leaguers who quit the majors to play in Japan. In 1962, Larry Doby and Don Newcombe, former Negro Leaguers who were among the first African-American players to reintegrate the majors, also became the first American players to sign on with the Japanese leagues. Many others followed, but most American sportswriters and fans believed that Japanese baseball was for American players when they got too old or were no longer good enough for the majors.

But Cecil Fielder gave people reason to reconsider these attitudes. After four years as a bench warmer for the Toronto Blue Jays, Fielder signed with the Hanshin Tigers, where he hit 38 home runs with 81 RBIs in just 106 games. The following year, he returned to American baseball with the Detroit Tigers. If the critics of Japanese baseball were right, Fielder would have faded into mediocrity. Instead, in his first three years back, he hit more home runs and collected more RBIs than any other major leaguer.

The Roots of the Revolution

The signing of Jackie Robinson did not suddenly change everything — in baseball, in other sports, or in society in general. Almost fifty years after his 1947 signing with Brooklyn, scouts for the Baltimore Orioles and Pittsburgh Pirates were claiming that because of "body types and genetics" Mexicans were not suited as position players in the majors, Cincinnati Reds owner Marge Schott received a lenient one-year suspension for making blatant racial slurs about African-Americans and Jews, and civil rights leader Jesse Jackson threatened to boycott and demonstrate unless the major leagues and all twenty-eight teams developed a plan to improve minority hiring in managerial and administrative positions.

Just as the signing of Jackie Robinson has not changed the attitudes and behavior of organized baseball overnight, neither did the inclination to integrate the big leagues occur overnight, as it seemed to many. By 1946 the momentum to topple the color line was nearly irresistible, but it had been building for some time — at least since the 1930s. That was the time of President Franklin D. Roosevelt's progressive politics, the anti-racist activism of the labor union movement, and the continuing campaign of the African-American newspapers, eventually joined by Jimmy Powers of the *New York Daily News*, Shirley Povich of the *Washington Post*, and other white sportswriters in calling for the fulfillment of Rube Foster's dream.

Roosevelt increased the momentum when he established the Fair Employment Practices Commission to blow the whistle on discriminatory hiring practices, and in 1945, after Americans of all colors were united for the sake of the war effort, the National Association for the Advancement of Colored People launched its "Double V" campaign to link victory over the racism of Nazi Germany with victory over racism in America. The NAACP specifically listed the integration of baseball as a step in the right direction. But if it were not for the giant steps taken by Joe Louis, the prizefighter whose immense popularity as heavyweight boxing champion cut across all racial and social lines, America may not have been ready for Jackie Robinson.

Knocking out Racism

Boxing, like basketball, was taken up avidly by the sons of European immigrants. Especially during the 1930s, when the economy stagnated and making a living seemed near impossible, many of America's urban poor turned to boxing. Many popular champions such as Max Baer and Barney Ross, Carmen Basilio and Rocky Graziano, and Tommy Loughram and James Braddock were also heroes in their respective Jewish, Italian, and Irish neighborhoods. But no champion was more popular or had more cross-cultural and interracial appeal than "the Brown Bomber," Joe Louis.

When Joe Louis knocked out James J. Braddock to win the heavyweight championship of the world in 1937, he was the first African-American to fight for the title since Jack Johnson in 1915. If Johnson traumatized white racists in America when he beat Tommy Burns in Australia in 1908 to become the first Black American heavyweight champ, then he literally drove the supremacists into violent despair on July 4, 1910, when he successfully defended his crown against Jim Jeffries.

Jeffries, a former champion who had retired undefeated, was called out of retirement by a mandate of people who could not and would not accept the fact that African-Americans were the athletic (or social) equals of European-Americans. For the occasion, Jeffries was dubbed "the Great White Hope," and in what must rank as one of the most socially significant boxing matches of all time, Johnson mercilessly beat Jeffries, mocking his ineffectiveness before knocking him out in the fifteenth round. In the race riots and mob violence against Blacks that broke out in cities across the U.S. following the fight, thirteen African-Americans were killed and hundreds were wounded. So violently did the racists react to this fight that distribution of the fight films was outlawed by Congress.

Joe Louis's reign as champion (1937-1949), the longest in boxing history, was far different than Jack Johnson's. Unlike Johnson, Louis was soft-spoken, and he didn't openly insult his opponents or detractors. Too, by the late '30s most Americans were united by concerns for the economy and too worried about threats of European military aggression to allow a minority of bigots to seize the spotlight. When Louis became champion, he rivaled Satchel Paige in popularity among African-Americans, and soon after he was a hero to nearly all Americans.

Very few sporting events had drawn as much attention as the 1938 Joe Louis–Max Schmeling boxing match for the heavyweight championship of the world. Although Louis and Schmeling would later become good friends, this bout was staged against a background of mounting international tensions and disturbing rumors of mass exterminations of Jews in Austria and Poland by Nazi soldiers. The Nazi position on race pushed to national extremes the bigotry that had segregated baseball and assailed Jack Johnson. Although Schmeling may never have been a very good Nazi, he was a German citizen, and most of America saw this bout as nothing less than a mythic contest of good versus evil.

And a frightening and dangerous contest it was, because evil just might win. Two years earlier Schmeling had handed Louis his only loss, a twelfth-round knockout heralded by the government in Germany as proof of the superiority of the Aryan race. But this time Louis was all over Schmeling from the opening bell, knocking him to the canvas four times in scoring a first-round knockout. The entire nation celebrated, and for the first time America

First African-American heavyweight champion Jack Johnson (top) enraged bigots; thirty years later Joe Louis (bottom) became a national hero to virtually all Americans.

In both his boxing and his life, Muhammad Ali's style has been called inspirational and outrageous.

had an African-American hero. There would be other popular African-American boxers after Louis, but none would carry the added burdens of social significance and political controversy into the ring with him until the era of Muhammad Ali.

A big man with incredibly fast hands, nimble feet, and crisp, powerful punches, Ali may have been the best heavyweight ever. The only man to win the heavyweight championship three times, Ali is best remembered for his fights with Joe Frazier, three of the most thrilling boxing matches ever witnessed. But Ali's most important contributions as a sports hero derive from his actions outside the ring. Like Jack Johnson, Ali was brash and outspoken, and he taunted his opponents. He would write poetry predicting the round in which he would knock out his rivals, and he often did exactly as he said he would. He made a recording called "I Am the Greatest." His style delighted some and outraged others.

But eventually he became too controversial for the sports establishment. He threw his Olympic medal into the Ohio River to protest prejudice and racial discrimination, and the day after he defeated Sonny Liston for the heavyweight crown in 1964, he declared his conversion to Islam and changed his name from Cassius Clay to Muhammad Ali. Though a few athletes and sports journalists came to his defense, Ali was increasingly criticized.

While the U. S. had come to accept African-American athletes and champions, Ali refused to limit his behavior to socially or racially acceptable images. A follower of Malcolm X, Ali risked his career and his freedom when in 1967 he announced his opposition to the Vietnam war and refused induction into the military. The World Boxing Association (WBA) promptly stripped Ali of his title and took away his license to box. Soon after, a federal court indicted him for draft evasion and sentenced him to five years in prison.

Ali never went to jail, and three years later the Supreme Court overturned his conviction on the grounds that the FBI had violated his civil rights with illegal wire taps. He resumed his boxing career and once again rose to the top of his sport. If Joe Louis prepared America for Jackie Robinson, then Muhammad Ali prepared America for even more. He taught the nation to accept African-American athletes for who they are: a varied group of individuals who will no longer comply with racist expectations that they play out their public personalities within a narrow range of "acceptable" roles. It was another important lesson in the ongoing revolution that grew out of the signing of Jackie Robinson.

Harsh Realities and the Field of Dreams

While Dodgers owner Branch Rickey staked his claim in history by signing Jackie Robinson, several team owners before him had taken a stab at baseball's color line. And while all were thwarted by then-commissioner Kenesaw Landis, each helped weaken the resistance of the defenders of the color line. It was thus Rickey and new commissioner Happy Chandler who finally knocked the mythical wall down.

Rickey, who had a brief career as a catcher at the turn of the century, combined the idealism of a committed integrationist with the hard-headed business sense of a savvy front-office baseball man. Rickey had been working very quietly on a plan to integrate the Dodgers since 1943. He did not share his plan with Commissioner Landis, a staunch defender of the color line. While pointing out that there was no written rule barring African-Americans from playing in the "white" majors, Landis variously claimed that there were no Black players good enough for the majors, that because of social segregation, travel arrangements would be impossible for integrated teams, and that white major leaguers would refuse to play with or against African-American players. Landis didn't live to see these objections overcome, not always easily, but overcome nevertheless. When Landis died in 1944, Rickey confided in the new commissioner, Happy Chandler, who made it clear that he would not oppose Rickey's plan.

A key part of the plan was to find the "right" man, and to do this Rickey organized an all-Black team, the Brooklyn Brown Dodgers, and hired the aging Oscar Charleston to manage. In reality, the Brown Dodgers were just a front so that Rickey's scouts could get a good, close look at the available Black talent. Nobody knew that they were really recruiting for the National League Brooklyn Dodgers.

When they found Jackie Robinson, they knew they had found the right man. Not only was Robinson a great all-around athlete, a fierce competitor, and an articulate, educated man who stood up for his rights, he had also grown up in a diverse neighborhood among Americans

In his ten years with the Brooklyn Dodgers, Jackie Robinson led them to six World Series.

of European, African, Mexican, and Japanese descent. Robinson attended integrated schools and competed on integrated college teams, where he was the subject of much publicity and not infrequent racial abuse. He was a non-drinker and non-smoker, a World War II veteran, and he had a stable marriage. And perhaps most important, Jackie Robinson had the character to face the pressures and abuses that he was sure to face, and channel his impulse to strike back into his on-the-field performance. It is sad that so much emphasis was placed on Robinson's image rather than his talent, and that tolerance became his responsibility. But Rickey believed, probably correctly, that a fight or an angry outburst would play into the hands of the anti-integrationists and set back the cause indefinitely.

Oddly, the Boston Red Sox almost beat Rickey to the punch. Under pressure from the Boston city council in 1945, the Red Sox hastily arranged a tryout for Negro League stars Jackie Robinson, Sam Jethroe, and Marvin Williams. By all accounts, the trio positively sparkled, drilling line drives off the wall and showing speed and grace on the field. But a don't-call-us-we'll-call-you was all they got for their efforts. The Boston Braves, who were under equal pressure to recruit African-American players, declined even to hold a tryout, although in 1950 Sam Jethroe would become the Braves' first Black

Requiem for the Negro Leagues

The 1947 East-West All Star game drew a huge, enthusiastic crowd of 48,000. The game featured five players — Monte Irvin, Minnie Minoso, Sam Jethroe, Quincy Trouppe, and winning pitcher Dan Bankhead — who would soon follow Jackie Robinson into the major leagues. But for Negro League team owners, the Jackie Robinson revolution not only began the process of bringing African-American players into the majors, it also drove African-American owners out of organized baseball.

For a while, African-American teams continued to serve as an unofficial minor league by developing prospects such as Ernie Banks and Hank Aaron and waiting for the major leagues to "discover" them. But in 1956, New York Cubans pitcher Pat Scantlebury was the last player signed directly from a Negro League team into the majors, and increasingly, talented African-American players went straight from high school to the integrated minor league farm system.

Negro League owners hoped that integration would come on a team-by-team basis. Because it did not, they were disappointed and financially ruined. Attendance dropped dramatically after 1947. When Satchel Paige left the Negro Leagues for the integrated majors, most fans left with him. After sixteen glorious years, the second Negro National League folded following the 1948 season. Although the Negro American League continued for a dozen more seasons, average salaries fell to a meager $200 per month, and games often featured decadent side show attractions in hopes of increasing attendance. The Indianapolis Clowns, whose last noble gesture was to deliver Henry Aaron to the Milwaukee Braves organization, became the kings of burlesque baseball, using donkeys and clowns in a game that only sadly resembled the grandeur of Pop Lloyd and Josh Gibson.

player. After passing up this chance to sign Jackie Robinson, the Red Sox shamefully stalled fourteen years before suiting up the switch-hitting infielder Pumpsie Green, so becoming the *last* team in the major leagues to integrate.

When Jackie Robinson was assigned to the Montreal Royals of the International League, no one predicted that he was bound for the Hall of Fame. Most of the baseball establishment, in fact, seriously underestimated his talent, doubting even his ability to play at the minor league level. But in his first game he collected four hits, including a homer, and stole two bases. Robinson was joined on the Royals by African-American pitchers John Wright and Roy Partlow. But as the first Blacks in the white leagues since 1898, Wright and Partlow could not hold up to the baiting and racial abuse, and they chose to return to the Negro Leagues. Robinson not only endured, he led the IL with a .349 batting average, tied for the lead in runs scored with 113, finished second in stolen bases with 40, and led the Royals to the league championship.

In every respect, as a player, as a man, and as a pioneer, Jackie Robinson proved he was ready to step up to the majors. During his rookie season with the Dodgers, he faced the verbal abuse of opposing players and the disrespect of some teammates, who threatened to strike unless "the Negro" was cut from the team (a blistering tongue-lashing from Brooklyn manager Leo "the Lip" Durocher set these renegades straight). He also endured hate mail from fans and even threats against his family. Despite these distractions, Robinson hit .297 with 29 stolen bases and 125 runs scored, winning the 1947 National League Rookie-of-the-Year award as the Dodgers won the pennant. Mean-

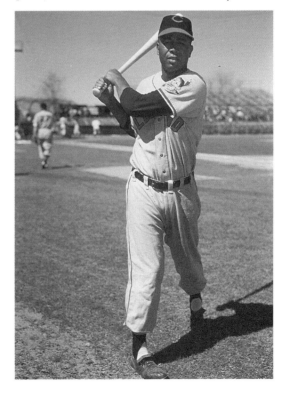

Larry Doby, the first African-American player in the American League since the nineteenth century.

while, before the season ended, three more African-Americans, Larry Doby of the Cleveland Indians and Henry Thompson and Willard Brown of the St. Louis Browns, appeared in the majors and another thirteen Blacks were playing in the minors. By 1949 there were thirty-six Black players in the major and minor leagues. The Jackie Robinson revolution had taken hold and would never be reversed.

Before he retired at the end of the 1956 season, Robinson had played every position except catcher and pitcher, compiled a .311 lifetime batting average, and led the Dodgers to six World Series in ten years. His best year came in 1949, when he won Most Valuable Player honors and knocked in 124 RBIs while leading the league in batting at .342 and in stolen bases with 37.

The first African-American inducted into the Hall of Fame, Jackie Robinson stands as the most important American athlete since World War II. We can measure his batting average. We can count his stolen bases. But every time he played, he helped tear down stereotypes and build African-American pride. We won't find that on the back of his baseball card, but those are achieve-

Two home runs for Hank Aaron

On September 23, 1957, the U.S. National Guard escorted African-American schoolchildren to school in Little Rock, Arkansas. These armed escorts were necessary to protect the children from mob violence at the hands of southern white racists who vehemently opposed school desegregation. That same day, young Henry Aaron hit the 109th home run of his major league career with two outs in the bottom of the eleventh off St. Louis Cardinal pitcher Billy Muffett. That blast won the game and the pennant for the Milwaukee Braves. Aaron went on to win the National League MVP that season, and eventually he became the major league all-time leader in home runs (755), RBIs (2,297), extra-base hits (1,477), and total bases (6,856). But that day, ten years after the reintegration of big league baseball and in stark contrast to the scene in Little Rock, Henry Aaron was carried off the field by his teammates, white and Black, the toast of the entire town of Milwaukee.

Sixteen years later, as he drew closer and closer to Babe Ruth's home run record, it was Aaron, now an Atlanta Brave, who needed the armed bodyguard.

Dear Hank Aaron,

Retire or die!... You'll be in Shea Stadium July 6-8, and in Philly July 9th to 11th..... You will die in one of those games. I'll shoot you in one of them.

Dear Hank,

... if you come close to Babe Ruth's 714 homers I have a contract out on you.... If by the all star game you have come within 20 homers of babe you will be shot on sight by one of my assassins....

Aaron's 109th home run symbolized the promise of shared joys and enrichments of integrated baseball. But when the segregationist legacy of 1887 reared its ugly head, that promise seemed broken. Throughout most of the 1973 season Hank Aaron received three thousand letters a day, most of it hate mail, and some of it containing death threats against Aaron and his family. He lived most of that season isolated from his teammates, surrounded by hired bodyguards, unable to enjoy the glory of becoming the home run king. Despite this pressure, Aaron finished the '73 season with a .301 batting average, 96 RBIs, and 40 homers. But his 40 home runs left him at 713, one short of tying Ruth and two shy of the all-time record.

Early the next season, on April 8, 1974, Hammerin' Hank stroked number 715.

A city bus pass welcomes "home" Hank Aaron, the Brave who made Milwaukee famous in the '50s and '60s. In 1975-77, Aaron played for the Milwaukee Brewers.

ments that have forever enriched baseball and America. Despite the immediate success of Jackie Robinson, Larry Doby, and others who first reintegrated the major leagues, most major league executives were slow to sign African-Americans to their squads. The integration of major league baseball took place by slow degrees and in the face of reluctance. For the first seven years, the majors added African-Americans at the rate of two per year, and it took until 1959, twelve years after Robinson debuted with the Dodgers, for Black players to make up about 14 percent of the major league rosters.

And no sooner were the leagues technically integrated than newer and subtler forms of discrimination appeared. Except for the Dodgers and Cleveland Indians, most teams seemed to abide by an unwritten rule that allowed no more than two African-Americans in the lineup at any one time. And most of the nonwhite players were outfielders and first basemen, with very few at the leadership positions of pitcher, catcher, or shortstop. And finally, after these grievances were eventually redressed, it remained to integrate coaching, management, and executive administration.

The first generation of African-American players to follow in Jackie Robinson's footsteps were remarkably good. By the mid-1950s, the Black position players had a batting average twenty points higher than the rest of the league. Roy Campanella, Robinson's teammate on the Brooklyn Dodgers, won the National League Most Valuable Player award three times in the 1950s before he was paralyzed from the chest down in an automobile accident. Winner of the 1956 Cy Young award Don Newcombe joined Campanella to form the first African-American battery in the majors. Larry Doby signed with Cleveland as a twenty-three-year-old directly out of the Negro Leagues and became the first African-American in the American League. In 1952 he led the league in homers with thirty-two. And Elston Howard, a catcher for the Yankees, was the first African-American on his team and the first to win the American League MVP.

In 1951, the New York Giants fielded the first all-African-American outfield of Hank Thompson, Monte Irvin, and Willie Howard Mays. Willie Mays could do it all. Along with Hank Aaron and Mickey Mantle, Mays was the premier home run hitter of the 1950s and 1960s. But he also led the league in stolen bases four times, and he played centerfield with a flair for the spectacular that won him twelve Golden Glove Awards.

Soon following Jackie Robinson's lead were the all-time greats Ernie Banks, Hank Aaron, and Frank Robinson. After coming up through the ranks of the Kansas City Monarchs, Ernie Banks played his entire nineteen-year career (1953-1972) with the Chicago Cubs. Known for his love of baseball, the slim-built shortstop was deceptively powerful. In the six years spanning 1955 through 1960, he hit more homers than Mantle, Mays, or Aaron. Hank Aaron, of course, spent twenty-three years in the majors, most of it in the shadow of more flamboyant stars like Willie Mays, quietly hitting more home runs than anyone else in major league history. Eight times he hit forty or more homers. Eleven times he drove in one hundred or more RBIs. Fourteen times he batted over .300. And he did all this in the era of integrated baseball, when he stepped up to the plate to face not just the best white pitchers, not just the best African-American pitchers, but the best pitchers in baseball.

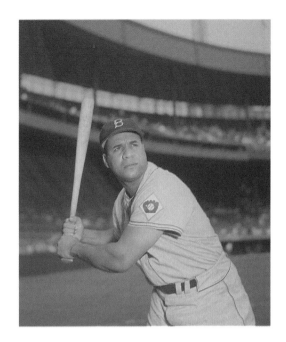

Top: Of mixed Italian-African-American descent, Dodger Roy Campanella was revered by fans on and off the field. *Bottom:* "Mr. Cub," Ernie Banks, was also a fan favorite.

Opening the Door to Management and Other Positions

A great player of the '50s and '60s, Frank Robinson became the first African-American player to win the triple crown when, in 1966, he led the American League in home runs, runs batted in, and batting average. And he is the only player ever to win the Most Valuable Player award in both the American and

Roberto Clemente and his legacy to Latin American ballplayers

The classic formula for superstardom for a position player is to excel in five areas: throwing, running, fielding, hitting, and hitting for power. If you add dignity, pride, grace, compassion, and a sense of humor, you have someone truly worthy of being a sports hero. You have, in fact, Roberto Clemente.

Clemente, an unorthodox batter who used a huge bat and stood as far away from the plate as he could, won four batting titles, had a career .317 batting average, played in fourteen All-Star games, won twelve Golden Glove Awards, and set a major league record by leading rightfielders in assists five times.

When asked how best to pitch to Clemente, Sandy Koufax, the great Dodger pitcher, suggested, "Roll the ball." Koufax's teammate Jim Brewer predicted, "Roberto Clemente will hit .320 the year after he dies." And Clemente's arm was so strong and so accurate that most runners simply stopped trying to take the extra base on him. Clemente was still going strong — in the 1972 season he batted .312 and collected the 3,000th hit of his career — when he died in a plane wreck on New Year's Eve, 1972, attempting to deliver relief supplies to earthquake victims in Nicaragua.

Clemente, born in Puerto Rico in 1934, played his entire career with the Pittsburgh Pirates, a team that had winced its way through three straight 100-loss seasons before Clemente joined them. Despite his accomplishments on the field, the national public and sportswriters were reluctant to give this Latin American the recognition he deserved. Even though he played 140 or more games every season from 1960 through 1967, sportswriters saddled Clemente with the labels of hypochondriac and slacker. In 1960, when the Pirates won the NL pennant and a thrilling World Series victory over the New York Yankees, Clemente hit .314 with 16 homers and a team-leading 94 RBIs, but he was snubbed in the MVP balloting, finishing eighth. Even more offensively, sportswriters would caricature Clemente's accent in print and make up quotes such as, "Me like hot weather, veree hot. I no run fast cold weather," which they

attributed to him. This was pure racism. Roberto Clemente never spoke like that.

The earthquake that hit Nicaragua on December 23, 1972, killed 10,000 and left 250,000 homeless. Roberto Clemente did not merely lend his name or donate money to the relief effort. He helped pack, stack, and load supplies onto the plane, and along with a small crew, he was one of five who accompanied the supplies on the ill-fated flight to Managua. The plane crashed shortly after takeoff. There were no survivors. Three months later, in a special election, the Baseball Writers Association of America elected Roberto Clemente to the Hall of Fame, the first Latin American player to receive this honor.

Clemente had often spoken of building a sports city in his homeland for Puerto Rican youth. After his death, a memorial fund helped establish the Roberto Clemente Sports City and a baseball school. This school has found and nurtured some of the best talent paying major league baseball today, including Roberto and Sandy Alomar, Benito Santiago, Ruben Sierra, Juan Gonzales, Ivan Rodriguez, and Carlos Baerga. Indeed, Latin American representation among major league rosters is a source of deep pride in Latin America and in the Latino communities of North America, and without exception, every one of today's Latin American stars has Roberto Clemente as a hero.

"If you have the opportunity to make things better, and you don't do that," Clemente said in a speech in 1971, "you are wasting your time on this earth." Roberto Clemente did not waste our time or his.

National Leagues. But Robinson truly left his mark on baseball history in 1975 when he became the first African-American major league manager. As early as 1962, the Cubs had hired Buck O'Neill, a Black coach, and Gene Baker had been appointed a minor league manager in 1961. In 1966, Emmett Ashford, who had fifteen years' experience umpiring in the minor leagues, became the first African-American umpire in the majors, and Robinson himself had managed winter ball in Puerto Rico for six years. But his appointment as manager of the Cleveland Indians was a big step. The Jackie Robinson revolution made progress against baseball's racist traditions, but it took twenty-eight years from the time baseball could accept a Black man on the field until it was ready for an African-American in charge of the team.

Leading the second wave of integration in baseball, Frank Robinson became the first African-American manager in 1975.

Robinson's lead opened the door for other Black and Latin Americans in management. In the early 1980s, Maury Wills piloted the Seattle Mariners. More recently, Hal McRae, Don Baylor, Felipe Alou, and Tony Perez were hired as major league skippers. And in 1992 Cito Gaston became the first African-American manager to win the World Series. Nearly fifty years after the start of the Jackie Robinson revolution, baseball is beginning to see integration in front-office and executive positions. Hank Aaron and Reggie Jackson now serve as vice presidents for the Atlanta Braves and New York Yankees respectively, and former player Bill White currrently serves as president of the National League.

During its years of segregation and since, major league baseball and its heroes have been a great source of enjoyment and pride for ethnic Americans. Connie Mack and John McGraw inspired Irish-Americans. Honus Wagner, Casey Stengel, Lou Gehrig, and Babe Ruth made German-Americans proud. Polish-Americans had Stan Musial and Ted Kluszewski, Italian-Americans had the DiMaggio brothers and Yogi Berra, and Jewish-Americans took deep pride in the heritage of Hank Greenberg and Sandy Koufax. Bob Gibson and Juan Marichal, Reggie Jackson and Dave Winfield, Darryl Strawberry and Rickey Henderson, Frank Thomas and Pat Listach — the list goes on — each has benefited from the struggles of Jackie Robinson and the other pioneers, and each in turn continues the tradition by inspiring their fans and future athletes. But before integration, Americans of color had to look for their heroes in separate leagues. They found their heroes, all right, but because they had to look in baseball's ghettoes, look even for the box scores in separate newspapers, the search itself was a constant reminder that they were excluded and cheated by a racist society. Since the reintegration of the game, all Americans, whether their heritage is African, European, Asian, or Latin American, can share pride in knowing that baseball is proof that prejudice can be overcome, that integration can work, and that diversity will enrich us all.

1858	First baseball league formed
1872	John "Bud" Fowler, first professional African-American baseball player, signs with the Cincinnati Red Stockings
1887	Superstar player-manager Cap Anson demands that African-Americans be banned from organized baseball leagues
1896	Basketball becomes a professional sport; in landmark decision (*Plessy v. Ferguson*), U.S. Supreme Court upholds states' right to enact laws requiring racial segregation
1906	Sol White's *The History of Colored Baseball* published
1906-10	Nine million Europeans emigrate to the United States
1910	Jack Johnson, first African-American heavyweight boxing champion of the world, successfully defends his title against the "Great White Hope," Jim Jeffries
1911	Cubans Armando Marsans and Rafael Almeida are signed by the Cincinnati Reds
1912	American Indian Jim Thorpe wins gold medals for both the pentathlon and decathlon in Olympics competition, gaining a reputation as the world's best athlete
1916	American Tennis Association founded to promote tournaments and provide facilities for African-Americans
1919	Jim Thorpe founds the first professional football league, the American Professional Football Association
1920	U.S. women get the right to vote; Rube Foster organizes the first Negro National League (baseball)
1922	Fritz Pollard becomes the National Football League's first African-American coach (Milwaukee Badgers)
1923	Eastern Colored League (baseball) organized
1926	United Golfers Association launched to sponsor tournaments for African-American golfers
1930	Rube Foster, the "father" of Negro League baseball, dies
1930-42	All-Jewish Philadelphia Sphas dominate the American Basketball League, winning six championships in twelve years
1932	All-African-American New York Renaissance Big Five basketball team wins eighty-eight straight games
1933	Negro National League reorganized by Gus Greenlee; first East-West All Star game
1934-46	African-Americans are banned from the NFL
1937	Negro American League (baseball) starts
1937-49	Joe Louis reigns as heavyweight boxing champion of the world
1939	New York Rens win the first World Basketball Tournament
1943-54	The All-American Girls Professional Baseball League (AAGPBBL)
1944	In contrast to the NFL, West Coast minor league football teams field integrated squads
1945	The Brooklyn Dodgers organization announces that it has signed Jackie Robinson and will assign him to play with their minor league club in Montreal for the 1946 season
1946-49	The Cleveland Browns, the most integrated team in the All-American Football Conference, win four straight AAFC championships
1947	Jackie Robinson plays with the Brooklyn Dodgers, reintegrating major league baseball and winning the National League Rookie-of-the-Year award
1949	The National Basketball Association begins its first season; there are no African-American players

76

1950	AAGPBBL directors prohibit women from becoming managers; Althea Gibson is the first African-American to play in the United States Lawn Tennis Association Nationals at Forest Hills; Chuck Cooper, Sweetwater Clifton, and Earl Lloyd integrate the NBA
1952	Major league baseball adopts rules barring women from signing as players
1954	Supreme Court rules (*Brown v. the Board of Education*) that public schools and school facilities must be available to all Americans regardless of race
1959	Boston Red Sox become the last major league baseball team to integrate; St. Louis Hawks become the last NBA team to integrate; Charlie Sifford becomes the first African-American golfer in the Professional Golfers Association
1962	The Washington Redskins become the last NFL team to integrate
1964	Cassius Clay defeats Sonny Liston to win the heavyweight boxing crown, then promptly announces his conversion to Islam and changes his name to Muhammad Ali
1970	The National Women's Football League is inaugurated
1972	Title IX of the Educational Amendments Act passes Congress and requires athletic programs to provide equal opportunities and benefits to men and women alike; Roberto Clemente dies in a plane crash while bringing relief aid to earthquake victims in Nicaragua
1973	Billie Jean King defeats Bobbie Riggs in a nationally televised "battle-of-the-sexes" tennis match
1974	Hank Aaron hits home run number 715, surpassing Babe Ruth to become the all-time home run king
1975	Frank Robinson becomes the first African-American manager in major league baseball (Cleveland Indians); Arthur Ashe wins Wimbledon and becomes the first African-American male rated number one tennis player in the world
1978	First season of the Women's Basketball League
1980	Doug Williams becomes the first African-American quarterback to start regularly for an NFL team
1984	Nancy Lieberman stars as the Women's American Basketball Association folds after its first year
1993	Arthur Ashe dies; Jesse Jackson negotiates with major league baseball executives, urging all twenty-eight teams to propose specific affirmative action plans for hiring minorities in front-office positions

GLOSSARY

African-American Press	informal network of newspapers serving Blacks throughout the U.S.; the only continuous voice calling for racial integration in sports and society throughout the 1920s, 1930s, and 1940s
anti-Semitism	hostility, prejudice, or discrimination against Jews
apartheid	practice or policy of segregating groups; the term is derived from South Africa's official policy of racial segregation and political, economic, and legal discrimination against non-whites
Ashkenazi Jews	the Jewish people from Eastern Europe
barnstorming	the practice by sports teams, usually basketball or baseball teams, of stringing a tour of one-night stands in small towns and cities to put together makeshift schedule of games
besoboru	the Japanese term for baseball; the Japanese have played professional baseball since 1934, and beginning with African-Americans Larry Doby and Don Newcombe, several hundred North American major leaguers have signed on with Japanese teams

Black Sox	derogatory name for the 1919 Chicago White Sox, eight members of which conspired with a gambler to purposely lose the World Series to the Cincinnati Reds
civil rights movement	a period beginning roughly in the mid-1960s marked by grassroots support and organized demonstrations calling for an end to racial discrimination in U.S. society
color line	unwritten rules that kept African-American and Black Hispanic players from participating in major league sports; most sports practiced at least token integration shortly after World War II
ERA (earned run average)	in baseball, the statistic representing the average number of earned runs scored against a pitcher for a game of nine full innings (twenty-seven outs); it does not include unearned runs scored as a result of fielding errors; an ERA is calculated by dividing the number of earned runs by the number of innings pitched, then multiplying by nine (for example, if a pitcher has pitched thirty-five innings and given up eight earned runs, his or her ERA is calculated by dividing 8 by 35, which equals approximately 0.229, and multiplying by 9, for an ERA of 2.06)
Negro Leagues	any of a series of baseball leagues operating from 1920 through 1960 and consisting of teams of African-American and Hispanic players; the Negro Leagues were organized in response to the racial segregation practiced in major and minor league baseball
RBI (run batted in)	in baseball, a run that is caused by a batter when a runner scores as a result of a hit, a sacrifice, a hit-by-pitch, or a base on balls (walk)
Rosie the Riveter	the personification of the patriotic U.S. woman during World War II who took an industrial job to support the war effort on the homefront
settlement house	community centers opened in ethnic neighborhoods during the wave of European emigration to the U.S. (1890-1920); most served as training grounds for ethnic-American athletes
stacking	steering athletes away from some positions and toward others because of their race

FURTHER READING

Allen, Maury. *Jackie Robinson: A Life Remembered*. New York: Franklin Watts, 1987.

Ashe, Arthur. *A Hard Road To Glory: A History of the African-American Athlete*, vols. 1-3. New York: Warner Books, 1988.

Bjarkman, Peter C. *Roberto Clemente*. New York: Chelsea House (Baseball Legends Series), 1991.

Cooper, Michael. *Playing America's Game: The Story of Negro League Baseball*. New York: Dutton/Lodestar, 1993.

Gardner, Robert and Shortelle, Dennis. *The Forgotten Players: The Story of Black Baseball in America*. New York: Walker, 1993.

Gregorich, Barbara. *Women at Play: The Story of Women in Baseball*. New York: Harvest/Harcourt Brace, 1993.

Levine, Peter. *Ellis Island to Ebbets Field: Sport and the American Jewish Experience*. New York: Oxford, 1992.

Macy, Sue. *A Whole New Ball Game: The Story of the All American Girls Professional Baseball League*. New York: Holt, 1993.

Menville, Chuck. *The Harlem Globetrotters*. New York: David McKay Co., 1978.

Nelson, Cordner. *Careers in Pro Sports*. New York: The Rosen Publishing Group, 1990.

Peterson, Robert W. *Cages to Jumpshots: Pro Basketball's Early Years*. New York: Oxford, 1990.

Rummel, Jack. *Muhammad Ali*. New York: Chelsea House (*Black Americans of Achievement* Series), 1988.